HOW TO IMPROVE WORKPLACE SAFETY

By Bryan McWhorter

Dragon Slayer Publishing

HOW TO IMPROVE WORKPLACE SAFETY
by Bryan McWhorter

© 2015, Bryan McWhorter, all rights reserved

Revised Jan. 2025

Editing by Linda Schlafer
Book Cover design by Michelle Ledet

Published in the U.S. by Dragon Slayer Publishing.

Paperback ISBN-13: 978-1530420100
ISBN-10:1530420105

Dragon Slayer Publishing

DEDICATION

This book is dedicated to all the heroes that work to keep people safe. From safety professionals and safety team volunteers to law enforcement, fire fighters, EMTs and those that serve in the military…Thank You!

How to Improve Workplace Safety

Table of Contents

How to Improve Workplace Safety

Introduction

"Making a living shouldn't have to cost you your life. Workplace fatalities, injuries, and illnesses are preventable. Safe jobs happen because employers make the choice to fulfil their responsibilities and protect their workers."
— Dr. David Michaels Assistant Secretary of Labor for Occupational Safety and Health

In 2013, 4,405 workers were killed on the job, according to the United States Department of Labor.

Employers are responsible for the safety of all employees as they perform their required duties. Safety is nothing to be lax about--it is much too important. If employers are going to be successful in keeping workers safe, they'll need a clear approach that is structured, proactive, and simple. This book was created for that very reason.

This book outlines a structured approach to improving safety that can be applied in any work environment. This material is based on the case study of an actual safety transformation that took place within the world's largest fluorescent light factory, Philips Lighting in Salina, Kansas.

Many of the safety activities we implemented to improve safety in this factory have been duplicated in factories around the world with similar results. The safety program I outline here will work for your company as well.

You don't work in a factory? No problem--the information provided here will work in any environment.

In 2008 I was assigned the position of Safety Officer at Philips Lighting. Our factory was experiencing an accident rate of three per week. Most were minor and required little attention. However, one of those accidents would be severe enough to require off-site medical attention, as in a trip to the hospital. Accidents were so common that they were accepted as just a normal part of working there.

I began working for Philips Lighting in August of 1986. In those days, our factory hired and trained people in groups, so several other new employees were in my orientation. I remember the Human Resources representative telling us that most likely one of us would get injured on our first day. This was based on his experience with new employees in the factory. He meant this as a warning for us to be on guard and be careful. He was correct, and I was the person that got hurt.

We produced fluorescent lamps from two feet to eight feet in length. All glass tubes were made in the glass department being drawn from a large furnace. The glass would be delivered to the coating department, where it was hand- loaded onto hangers on a moving conveyor chain.

I was standing on a platform with another new employee as we worked together side by side, hanging four-foot glass tubes. The person working beside me grabbed a broken tube of glass off the skid of glass we were loading, not noticing that the end of the glass tube was broken and jagged. He accidentally brought the jagged edge into contact with my right arm as he went to hang it. This gave me my first laceration from glass in my new job, on my first day!

The injury was minor, requiring only cleaning (important to make sure no glass remained in the wound) and a bandage. No one likes getting hurt or causing injury to another. Neither of us wanted this type of attention on our first day.

Fast forward to 2008, and accidents were still common. Nothing had changed regarding safety over the 22 years since I was hired! This was not for lack of trying on the part of Philips or our management team. I have seen and even been part of many safety initiatives as we tried all the typical approaches.

We formed safety committees and mentioned safety in town hall meetings and newsletters. We provided scratch cards that could be redeemed for prizes and tried other incentives for being safe. Nothing worked.

We faced the cold hard truth. We did not know how to effectively improve safety. If admitting you have a problem is the first step on the road to recovery and improvement, we were there.

We decided to start from scratch and infuse safety into all that we did. The safety program we created was successful. In 2009, we achieved a 50% reduction in OSHA recordable accidents over 2008. This was our goal, and we challenged all departments to reduce their accidents by 50%.

In 2009, we identified 545 safety projects with the help of the hourly workforce. In 2010, over 600 were identified. By the end of 2010, we had completed over 1,000 safety projects as we continued to reduce accident rates.

We developed a structure that worked for us, and it will work for your work environment as well. The steps are not complicated, but they do require commitment to safety. Safety must be number one.

When I say safety must be number one, I sometimes get push back and have been told that I am naive. "No management team will ever put safety over profit" was a statement I heard a lot. These people simply did not understand that embracing safety will improve profit.

Companies that recognize their employees as their strongest asset build loyalty and a workforce that is engaged and energized. Employee engagement is not only the key to workplace safety…it is the key to a successful business.

The fundamental truth is that we need each other. There is no such thing as a self-made man or woman. We rely on each other. When managers make decisions that are not in the best interest of the people they work with (employees, suppliers and customers), they degrade their businesses' overall effectiveness. I will talk more about this later.

In the first few sections of this book, I talk about human nature and why it is so difficult to keep people safe. It seems we truly are our own worst enemies. We will look at leadership and the culture needed for driving safety. People must be viewed as important and not as expendable commodities. A workplace environment should provide a sense of community.

Only after addressing the above topics will, I go into the actual steps we took to improve safety in our workplace and how we upgraded all aspects of our health and safety programs.

Please read it with an open mind. I promise you'll find ideas and activities you can implement to improve your work safety. You will adopt a mindset for driving safety in a sustainable way.

You will learn how to create an effective safety culture. All you must do is keep reading. I will outline everything for you, all based on firsthand experience.

CHAPTER 1

Big Problem

As I stated in the introduction, we admit we had a big problem when it came to keeping workers safe. Our factory was known for having a high injury rate.

In August of 2008, I was asked to take over the safety program for the manufacturing facility where I worked. I was the Senior Trainer for a large fluorescent lamp factory. In my position, I provided all the classroom training for our Lean Manufacturing Program (Continuous Improvement). I also created and facilitated classes on Leadership, Teamwork, Safety, and various aspects of our production system.

Our manufacturing facility was owned by Philips, a global company. The site was the world's largest manufacturer of fluorescent light bulbs. Close to 500 employees worked in this hazard-rich environment.

Our factory was unique in being fully automated. If everything worked as it should, no human hands ever touched the product. From when it was made into glass from sand to where the components of the fluorescent lamps were assembled and packaged, the automated equipment did it all.

The production mechanics took care of the equipment, and the equipment produced the fluorescent lamps. From a safety perspective, this presented many challenges.

Our factory has high-speed equipment with lots of moving parts. Our high-speed production lines produced thousands of fluorescent lamps each hour. The production line equipment could grab, pinch, crush, and lacerate. Our production processes also used very high heat and open flames, which were burn hazards.

The glass used to make the long lamps (some up to eight feet in length) was a constant laceration hazard. In short, this was the perfect environment in which to get hurt and people did get hurt quite often.

To add further difficulty in safety, our employees worked long hours, often in extreme heat. During the summer months, many areas of the factory floor could reach temperatures of over 120 F. Most of our employees worked twelve-hour shifts, with four crews of approximately 100 people per shift.

The work weeks would alternate between three and four days. One week they would work four days and the following week three days, in continuous rotation.

It was not uncommon for employees to work overtime for long stretches. I remember a year when as a production mechanic, I worked almost three months straight of twelve-hour days. It was not uncommon for employees to work twelve-hour days for long stretches in a row without a day off. Fatigue and complacency due to working long hours was a constant safety concern.

When I was approached about taking over safety, I was told that our headquarters wanted all sites to have a Safety Officer to drive a proactive safety program. I had been on safety teams in the past that tried to improve safety, so I was happy to put on the new hat as the Safety Officer. It also meshed well with my current position as the senior trainer. I would be responsible for all safety training.

What I did not know at the time was how many accidents we were racking up. I was happily clueless as to how bad our safety record was and learned that ignorance truly is bliss. It was information that turned my thoughts from "O boy!" to "O God!"

At that time, our facility was experiencing three accidents per week, and typically one of those was bad enough to require off-site medical attention, making it an OSHA Recordable accident. I was amazed to learn that our factory had one of the highest injury rates of all our companies' factories, worldwide!

After reviewing our safety stats, I remember visiting a friend who worked in Human Resources and telling him about our accident rate. I told him it was like we were running a lottery from hell. Three of our friends on the factory floor were going to get hurt this week, and we were just waiting to see who they were. The hair on the back of my neck stood up, I felt so helpless.

Our Current State of Safety

The first step in driving any change is always to understand the current condition.

Our factory had been in operation since 1967. By 2008, we had racked up forty-one years' worth of bad habits working with glass, fire and high-speed equipment.

I was told in my new hire orientation to expect one of us newbies to get hurt on our first day. (This was me) Injuries were expected. We did not have a safety culture, we had a performance culture, and accidents were accepted as normal. Performance was our number one priority, measured by high production levels, low equipment downtime and low scrap rates.

We had forty-one years of history stating we could not control safety. We were a shining example of what not to do regarding worker safety. It is difficult to drum up support for a program with that level of epic failure.

As a factory, we had bought into learned helplessness about safety. No one really believed we could improve worker safety.

As long as I can remember, management encouraged us to work safely. We tried many different safety initiatives and programs. The company spent thousands of dollars on safety prizes and incentives. We always ended up back at square one with blood on the floor.

Three people per week get hurt! We needed to break this cycle and do it quickly, but how? We have always had a safety team and safety initiatives. They just weren't ever successful, not even close.

Here are a few of the approaches we took to improve safety:

- We gave prizes for worker safety.

- We had people fill out a form whenever they found an unsafe condition.

- We had monthly safety meetings with a mix of hourly and salary employees.

- We promoted safety in Town Hall meetings. (Safety took a back seat to the main agenda items made up of production efficiency and profit/loss).

These efforts all had one thing in common, they weren't working!

Our greatest asset at that time was a management team and company that really did care about worker safety. They were concerned and committed to doing whatever it took to turn this around.

In the pro-column, we had passion, determination, caring and commitment. In the con- column, none of us had any experience in improving workplace safety, as our safety stats proved. We had to start at ground zero and build a new safety program from scratch.

I had enough conversations with HR and our management team to know they cared about employee safety. They were willing to try almost anything at this point. We were known in our town and with Philips globally as a dangerous place to work. This is not the reputation we wanted.

We knew we needed to get everyone involved in creating a completely different culture regarding safety. We needed management to lead the way. We needed everyone's engagement at all levels of the factory. This would not be easy.

We had to create a different mindset about safety. In the next chapter, I will tell you about "Dragon Slayers" and why we need everybody to be one.

CHAPTER 2

The Story of the Dragon Slayer

A long time ago in a kingdom far away, there was a castle. In this castle was a dragon slayer, for this kingdom had many dragons nearby that provided a constant threat, as is often the case with mythical kingdoms. The castle also had a dragon lookout that would keep watch and sound the alarm whenever a dragon was spotted heading towards the castle.

One morning, the dragon lookout sounded the alarm: "One dragon heading towards the castle!" Our brave slayer grabbed his sword, jumped on his trusty steed, and charged out the front gate. Clashing with the dragon, our hero was victorious, quickly cutting off the dragon's head.

Returning to the castle, he was greeted by the cheers of the people. Confetti flew, musicians played…they even fired up the gas grills and tapped some kegs. It was a grand celebration! Hurrah for the dragon slayer!

The next morning, our hero woke a little hung over from the previous night's celebration. He hadn't even finished flossing his teeth when he heard the dragon lookout's alarm: "Two dragons heading toward the castle!" Our hungover hero grabbed his sword and jumped on his horse to face the threatening dragons.

Once again, our hero was victorious. He easily dispatched the two dragons. Heading back to the castle, he was once again greeted by the cheers of the people. Confetti was thrown, music played, the gas grill was fired up, and more kegs were tapped.

As our brave knight enjoyed the festivities, he hadn't even made it through the salad bar before he heard the cry of the lookout, "Three dragons heading towards the castle."

Our hero put down his plate and mounted his horse to do battle again. Charging the three dragons, he fought bravely, but he was tired, hungry, and still hungover. He got bit a few times, but won in the end, after all, he is our story's hero.

Riding back towards the castle, our slayer thought to himself "Why do I have to do all the fighting? Why can't we have a few more slayers? Am I the only one that can pick up a sword?"

As he approached the front gate, he heard the dragon look-out sound the alarm, "Four dragons heading toward the castle."

Our hero turned his horse around and drew his sword to face another battle. Charging the dragons, his head throbbing now from his hangover, his empty tummy growling, our knight fought more out of frustration and anger than for the noble cause of protecting the kingdom. Once again, he was gnawed on, but won in the end, killing all four dragons.

Now back at the castle, our slayer tied up his horse and walked over to the festivities that were winding down. The gas grill was cold, and the steaks were gone. The band was putting up their amplifiers and the kegs stood empty.

Our hero once again heard the alarm, "Five dragons heading towards the castle!" Without blinking, our brave slayer drew his sword, walked over to the dragon lookout and cut off his head.

What is the moral to this story? There are too many dragons for one slayer to handle! This leads to someone losing their head.

In many of the work environments I have visited, there was one dedicated person driving safety. This was often the safety manager or safety officer. When this is the case, like the hero in our dragon slayer story, she or he will be very frustrated as the odds are greatly stacked against them.

In a large work environment of any type, hazards surface like dragons and one slayer is not enough. We need to train all workers in the basics of safety. If workers understand how to identify hazards and the possible risks, they can help drive safety. We need to make everyone a dragon slayer.

The front-line workers will notice unsafe conditions and behaviors before management, they deal with them daily. It does not matter what the work environment is, a restaurant, construction site, factory, retail store, farm, or hospital. Those that do the work know the issues. They see the dragons before anyone else does. They are already dragon lookouts.

We want to identify the dragons while they are baby dragons. (Safety issues) Those that do the work will see them first.

Prior to 2009, at our Philips Lighting factory, we had one person responsible for all safety efforts. This was the Safety Manager. When I was assigned the Safety Officer position in 2008, the Safety Manager position was vacant. Our Safety Manager had quit a year earlier, and we had not filled the position.

I remember visiting with our Safety Manager on many occasions before he left us for other pursuits. On one visit, I was sitting across the desk from him and noticed a stack of papers. When I asked him what they were, he told me they were forms employees filled out and turned in whenever they found something unsafe.

I don't know how many of these forms were on his desk, but it was a nice stack of identified dragons!

He saw the look of surprise on my face and said, "I know, right? What do they expect me to do?" He felt overwhelmed and helpless. He was one person with no one directly reporting to him who could help.

He let department heads know about the identified safety problems, but for the most part, nothing ever changed. Everyone had their own problems, and safety issues were low on the list. I believe the department heads cared about their people, but performance was king, and they did not understand the importance of dealing quickly with safety concerns. Especially in a factory with so many safety concerns. We became complacent regarding worker safety.

We needed to train everyone to slay dragons. Safety had to be everyone's concern, not just that of the Safety Manager. We are our brother's and sister's keepers. We are a community and protecting each other is an essential part of being a community.

We look out for each other. In 2009, we started training all employees in hazard identification. We kicked this off with a full day of safety training. We gave them a framework for addressing identified hazards and incentives for correcting them. I believe training is the most important aspect of your safety program. How much time and money do you spend on annual safety training? Employees recognize that management spends money on what is important. How important is worker safety to your management team?

Paradigm Shift

There is evidence provided by positive phycology backing up Henry Ford's statement "Whether you think you can or you think you can't, your right." Our beliefs can create a self-fulfilling prophecy. In our facility, we had a high level of learned helplessness regarding safety. An acceptance of injuries as normal came from years of failed safety programs and high injurie rates. We needed to change this view.

While reviewing our accident records, I uncovered something fascinating. Several employees have worked in our factory for many years injury free. These employees had no serious injuries requiring outside medical attention. Some had worked in our facility for over twenty years.

I interviewed many of them and found that they were dragon slayers. They had a high level of respect for their safety and the safety of those around them. They made it a habit to always follow safety rules. Many of them stated that they saw safety as a mark of professionalism. Master craftsmen work safely. I heard statements like "If you want to be able to keep working and earning a living, safety has to be number one." They were not safe by accident; they had a different mindset regarding safety. I asked several of them if I could use them as safety role models. All of them agreed to allow me to use them as proof that we could work in our factory and remain injury free.

These employees were instrumental in shifting from our learned helplessness perspective of "injuries are normal." I was able to show examples of individuals that worked in our factory for over twenty years and have never experienced a severe injury. If they can work injury free, so can you. This had a big impact on all of us. Here is proof that we can stay safe while working here. This created a paradigm shift regarding our view on working safe.

RACI

RACI stands for Responsible, Accountable, Consulted, and Informed. It's an acronym used to identify and define the roles and responsibilities of employees. We used this to make sure all employees understood their roles and responsibilities regarding worker safety. Everyone must be responsible for their own safety.

Responsible: All employees were responsible for their personal safety. Each employee was responsible for following all safety rules and making safety the number one priority. They were also responsible for addressing unsafe behaviors and conditions in their workplace.

Accountable: Managers, supervisors, and anyone in a leadership role were accountable for making sure safety rules were followed and unsafe conditions and behaviors were addressed quickly. They must be role models regarding safety.

Consulted: As the safety officer, I was consulted anytime there was an issue regarding safety that employees were not sure how to address. I was responsible for making sure we were compliant with OSHA and that our employees had the training, equipment, support and resources to work in a safe manner. Management was also consulted regarding all safety concerns.

Informed: We created flow charts showing steps to take and who to inform based on the event. This outlined who to contact and inform when there was an accident, near miss, etc. We also went to great lengths to make sure ALL employees were informed about our safety key-performance indicators and relevant information such as:

- Injuries and all relevant information about the injury.
- All near misses and information regarding them.
- Identified unsafe conditions and behaviors.
- Current safety projects.
- Health and safety concerns and information.

- Safety successes.

It was important for all employees to take ownership for their safety. This was particularly important as our goal was to equip all employees with the knowledge and support, they needed to work safely. We wanted everyone to be a safety expert regarding their work tasks and environment. We needed dragon slayers.

CHAPTER 3

Danger and Why We Run toward It!

People don't want to get hurt, but they don't want to fail. We will often put ourselves at risk physically to protect ourselves emotionally.

Humans are unique in that we don't typically run from danger. In fact, looking at our lifestyles and history, we often run toward danger. When we see a problem, our most likely response is to quickly intervene. We move instantly to catch a falling object or stop something from rolling away. Our bodies get us into trouble before our brains realize the bad situation we are in.

When our ancestors had to bring down a woolly mammoth to eat and survive, that's what they did; danger was a more acceptable risk than starvation. We do what we must.

When we are young, we seem to be wired to believe "I won't get hurt." We often think that even when we know there is danger, nothing bad will happen to us. We are invincible.

"After all," we tell ourselves, "I have faced dangerous circumstances before without getting hurt. I have lived this long even though I ride a motorcycle without a helmet, drive my car with worn-out tires, and drive a little too fast on icy roads. We take risks and we come out okay. No big deal.

Our children follow our example, though we tell them to do otherwise. Even worse, we may encourage them to take risks. We foster and encourage the little daredevil that's in all of us. We train our children to take risks.

When playing sports such as American football, we are told when injured to "shake it off and get back in there." We hear sayings like; "blood makes the grass grow" and "pain goes away, but glory lasts forever."

You will never hear a high school football coach tell his team to get out on the field and "play safe." We wear scars as badges of honor. Athletes want to prove how fearless and tough they can be, and we wonder why safety programs fail? It's amazing any succeed!

We tend to be competitive by nature. If we run equipment on a shift, we want to out-perform the other shifts. In manufacturing, if your shift has the highest production yield and the lowest scrap rate, life is good. You are emotionally safe so you can stand tall, respected for your expertise.

Most of us want to be admired for our work skills. Physical safety may not even be a factor we give much attention to. Physical safety can easily take a back seat to emotional safety.

A physical risk is often more acceptable than an emotional one. We need to feel respected and in control. We want to succeed at what we're responsible for.

Let's look at what motivates us. Why do we do the things we do?

The Motivational Triad

In the book, The Pleasure Trap, by Douglas J. Lisle and Alan Goldhamer, the authors explain the motivational triad.

The three motivations that dictate everything we do are:
- The desire for reward

- The avoidance of pain

- The conservation of energy

In the workplace, these factors influence safety. In-the-moment, we are often driven by our impulses, feelings and emotions. The three motivations are running the show.

The Desire for Reward

In a numbers/performance driven culture, the desire for reward is fulfilled by hitting our performance targets. We willingly take physical risks to protect ourselves emotionally and go for the desired reward.

All of us want to succeed in whatever we do. The more important the goal, the stronger the desire to succeed. "Whatever it takes" are words we hear too often. Risks can quickly become acceptable and encouraged.

For a mechanic on the shop floor, being judged against other mechanics operating the same equipment on another shift, safety may not be considered. What registers is GETTING THE JOB DONE! If we must take risks by repairing equipment "on the fly" (i.e., while it is running), then we do it. Protect the numbers. If your production numbers are better than the other mechanics, you win.

This was our work culture and had always been our culture prior to 2009. We talked about safety, but all our support was behind getting work done. We would tell mechanics to be safe while expecting them to perform tasks that were not safe.

Is it any wonder that the mechanics didn't believe management when they said from now on, we want them to think "Safety First"? This was a180 degree turn from our normal culture.

Our employees took a great deal of pride in achieving good production numbers and achieving set targets. They were very creative when it came to finding solutions for equipment that was running poorly.

Our mechanics knew the equipment inside out and had lots of experience in doing "whatever it took" for a good production yield while minimizing scrap and equipment down time.

To get a mechanic that had been working under this mindset for twenty or thirty years to change mental gears and put safety first was going to be a tough sell. Many of my friends on the factory floor told me flat out that it wouldn't happen. The production numbers had always come first and always would be first.

Let's continue looking at our motivational triad by looking at how we avoid pain.

The Avoidance of Pain

The avoidance of pain does not play in our favor for safety, either. Remember that feelings, impulses and emotions drive our actions from moment to moment. We will often choose to avoid emotional pain at the risk of physical pain.

Emotional pain is inflicted in a performance culture by not hitting the targets. A mechanic does not want to explain why the equipment is down or running poorly, so risks are taken. End of story.

Our factory was made up of high-speed production lines, which meant that a lot of money could be lost quickly if the equipment was running poorly. If a mechanic consistently had low production numbers such as high scrap or low product yield, she/he could risk demotion or even lose their job.

A manufacturing environment can be very dehumanizing. Since people are measured by production numbers, the equipment takes on their identity. If the equipment is running well, they are well; if the equipment is running poorly, their very job may be at risk.

Many of our workers felt that if a lead mechanic or supervisor told them to "work safe" and "put safety first," it is code for "Do whatever it takes, just don't tell me about it." This put the mechanic in a horrible position.

Let's look at our final motivator, the conservation of energy.

The Conservation of Energy

The conservation of energy, the last of our three motivators, is always at play. We tend to take short cuts whenever we can. We all fight laziness. Doing anything the safe way often requires extra effort. If it is not valued in the existing culture, why bother? Just find a way to get it done.

Using Lock out tag out, chalking tires, putting on personal protective equipment, going to get the right tools... all these things take effort, and if safety is not valued, no extra effort will be given. Even worse, there can be peer pressure from co-workers. If you are the only one performing a task the safe way, you will catch flack and lots of it!

Our production culture of 2008 had no chance of producing a successful safety program. Like dropping a freshwater fish into a salt-water tank, it was going to die and die quickly. Our work culture had to be changed. We need to change how everyone viewed safety. We needed top-down commitment and bottom-up support.

Safety First Means People First

In our facility we began placing more emphasis on our employees over all health and wellbeing. We widened our perspective beyond safety. This was done by:

- Annual health fairs and focusing on health and wellbeing beyond just safety.
- Fitness competitions. (Our facility had a small gym, baseball diamond and half mile walking track.)
- Creating a team and community mindset.
- Monthly health and wellness topics (Cancer awareness, smoking cessation, Heart health, etc.)
- A focus on leaders acting as coaches rather than bosses.
- Promoting a moral safety compass. Caring about each other's safety and protecting coworkers.

I am seeing this approach more and it excites me. I have noticed a trend lately. I have heard people make the statement "People first," rather than saying "safety first." The first time I heard someone make this statement while listing the business objectives, it gave me chills. The manager outlined the company focus as:

1. People
2. Quality
3. Cost
4. Delivery

This is brilliant and worth thinking about. What good is it to protect employees physically only to harm them mentally and emotionally? Safety is too limited unless it includes the whole person. There is more to us than our physical safety. We can protect the body and still harm the person. This is the primary reason why we see disengagement, quiet quitting, and high turnover. People do not quit companies, they quit other people that make them feel insignificant. They do not mind work, but do not like the workplace. This has been validated by the Gallup organization.

The average person does not complain about work and does not mind working. According to a 120-country study by the Wellbeing for Planet Earth Foundation and Gallup, more than 80% of the world's workforce enjoy their work. In these studies, people often state that they would continue to work even if they did not need the money. If more than 80% of people enjoy their work, then why are nearly 60% of workers quietly (Or actually) quitting? As reflected by information from the Gallup organization in 2022.

Dissatisfaction comes not from work, but from how workers feel they are treated. To feel secure, we must feel safe on three levels:
1. Emotional Safety
2. Professional Safety
3. Physical Safety

Level One – Emotional Safety
We will put ourselves at risk physically to protect ourselves emotionally. We don't like admitting failures. No one likes explaining mistakes or how we failed at a work task or to meet a set performance goal.

In the work environment, emotional safety means employees feel valued. They see themselves as part of a work family, community or team. They are treated with respect and as more than just a function.

When we know managers care about us, we are aware they would not want us to take risks. When we see they value us, including our safety, so will we. We may not like to admit it, but our sense of self-worth is influenced by how others perceive us. If we see management as friends that care about our emotional well-being, we know they care about our physical well-being as well. If they don't care about our emotional well-being, why would they care about our physical well-being? This is a big lack of congruency.

Level Two – Professional Safety

Most of us like being respected for what we do. We want to be known as that employee that can "get-r-done."

Our work is our livelihood. It is how we provide for our families. We will often take physical risks over losing our jobs due to bad performance. When we feel our job security may be at stake, we may take unnecessary risks to protect our employment.

We may use shortcuts such as not taking the time to get the right tools or putting on PPE. We may decide not to chalk tires or to use a fall arrest system when working at an elevated height. Safety almost always requires extra time and effort. If we feel that performance goals are more important to management than our safety, the extra time and effort may not be given.

Employees need to feel valued as part of the team. They need to feel secure that a mistake is not going to get them fired or demoted. Many companies such as Toyota, Next Jump, Barry-Wehmiller, Procter and Gamble, and Southwest Airlines have done an excellent job of establishing that their employees are their number one asset. Toyota management has stated they will not fire an employee for bad performance. They site performance issues as correctable by training and designing better ways of working. They want employees to succeed.

Level Three – Physical Safety

Only when workers know management cares about them emotionally and professionally will they believe management cares about their safety. The first two levels serve as a litmus test to employees regarding loyalty from management. If we do not feel safe in the first two levels, why believe management means it when they say, "work safe?"

We need to create a work culture where employees feel valued and protected on all three levels. Without the first two, level three will most likely not happen. However, when workers feel valued and protected, physical safety is naturally accepted even if not stated. It just makes sense.

We are fully engaged at work when all three levels of safety are in place. When you think about it, this makes perfect sense. The best we have to offer is not from our back and hands, but from our mind and heart. You can hire someone to show up, but if you want their loyalty, trust, full engagement, and resourcefulness, you must earn it. As Dr. John Maxwell is fond of saying, "People do not care how much you know, until they know how much you care."

Shareholder Value VS Stakeholder Value

In the same manner that we need to consider the whole person while thinking about safety, we need to consider the whole business or organization when making decisions regarding the overall wellbeing of the business. We need to broaden our focus beyond just profit. This is a perspective of stakeholder value rather than shareholder value.

All businesses are in a three-part symbiotic relationship made of employees, suppliers, and customers:

1. **Employees** are your work family and team. They meet the needs of the customers.
2. **Suppliers** are your business partners. You need them to be profitable so you can stay profitable.
3. **Customers** are who you serve with your goods and services.

Any decision you make that harms one of these groups harms your business. The litmus test for good business decisions is to make decisions that benefit all three. The world's best organizations see 72% of their workforce engaged. What if all organizations followed their example and strived to create great places to work?

In 2019, the largest companies in the U.S. came together and announced that they were no longer "shareholder capitalists," but instead, "STAKEHOLDER capitalists." They want a kind of capitalism that works for a range of constituencies -- including employees and communities -- and not just shareholders and the super-rich. – Gallup.

What would happen if this became mainstream? Imagine the largest companies building workplaces where employees thrive, suppliers are treated fairly, and customers are proud to support your organization? This type of organization would make everyone happy. Shareholders would reap the rewards of high productivity and profits and stakeholders such as employees would enjoy better physical and mental health.

The Evolution of Safety

This is a progression in the evolution of safety based on values. Does your organization value people as much as profit? Studies show that the two go hand in hand. Valued employees contribute to profitable and sustainable companies. We all want our companies to be profitable. Profitable businesses help the community. "A rising tied lifts all boats." However, profit should never come at the expense of stakeholders. Your stakeholders want the company to be profitable and will work hard to make it profitable if they are valued.

People First rather than safety first is a progression in safety management and the next step in the evolution of worker safety. It is widening our scope of concern beyond physical safety to include mental health and to recognize all three levels of safety: Emotional, professional, and physical. From an operation perspective, we shift focus from shareholder value to stakeholder value. We recognize our company's impact on the individuals we work with and the communities we serve.

So how about your company? Are you a "people first" company that focuses on stakeholder value over shareholder value? Seek to create a company that serves people and community. After all, your employees, suppliers and customers all happen to be people. Stakeholder focus provides the win/win/win.

"People first" makes total sense. Embracing a narrow perspective of just physical safety is like saying, "We care about your physical safety, we just don't care about you."

The Moral Safety Compass

A good friend and safety mentor once summed up the management dilemma of safety verses performance. As we walked across our factory floor, we saw an employee standing on a large piece of equipment. The equipment was about the size of a garden shed and not designed for anyone to be on top of it. My friend pointed at the employee and said, "Would you allow your adult son or daughter to perform these unsafe tasks? If not, then don't let your employees do them either. Find a way to make them safe."

This became our moral safety compass. If you would not let a loved one perform a dangerous work task, don't let anyone perform it. That is a clear and easy to understand safety level. It became our litmus test for activities. Energy and extra effort are required for worker safety. For safety to have a chance of taking hold, it must come first. When dilemmas arise (as they will) between safety and work goals, safety must win every time. We need to find a safe way to achieve our targets.

CHAPTER 4

Danger versus Hazard

While equipping our employees through safety training, we spent a lot of time and energy on creating a strong distinction between hazards and dangers. A person can work around hazards all day long, day after day without ever being in danger. If there is a safety device (control measure) in place for each hazard, and the control measures are used, there is no danger.

Here are some examples of control measures for identified hazards:
- Guards for moving equipment.

- Guards for extremely hot surfaces or open flames.

- Proper railing for raised platforms.

- Harnesses and fall protection for working where falling is a risk.

- Lock out tag out for energy hazards.

- Personal protective equipment such as earplugs for loud noise, etc.

- Proper safety training for competency in performing work in a safe manner.

You get the idea. If the hazard has been identified and the risk associated with it, and a control measure is put in place, there need not be any exposure to danger.

Control the hazard/risk and you remove danger.
1. Identify all hazards

2. Identify the risks associated with each hazard
3. Create control measures to prevent risks
4. Train anyone that could be exposed to the hazard

It's funny how we can look at safety standards differently at work than we do at home. For instance, it can be acceptable in work environments to be exposed to the danger of hazards without good control measures in place. In our personal lives, we would be offended if someone even hinted that we should subject our families, friends or ourselves to an identified danger.

Here is an example of what I mean. In 2008, it was acceptable, or at least taken for granted, that we were going to have three injuries each week. A worker on the shop floor knew that there was a good chance she could be injured just by going to work. If I knew that family members or visiting friends often got hurt in a certain part of my house, I would not allow them to go there! The acceptable injury rate in my house is zero!

Employees trained in safety understand that if control measures are in place for identified hazards, danger need not be an issue. The next step was to have all employees trained in how to identify various hazards in their work areas and make sure a control measure was in place.

They needed to understand how to perform hazard identification and risk assessment. We trained all employees on how to perform a hazard assessment. For each identified hazard what is the risk?

Examples of hazards and associated risks:

- Exposed electrical wire - Risk of electric shock

- Slippery surface - Risk of falling

- Uneven walking surface – Risk of tripping

- No rail on raised platform - Risk of falling from raised level

- No guard on moving equipment - Risk of being caught by moving parts

- Working in hot environments – Risk of heat related illnesses

- Exposure to loud noises – Risk of hearing loss

- Exposed harp edge – Risk of lacerations

We wanted our employees to SEE THE RISK. When a hazard is recognized by an employee, we wanted them to realize the risk associated with it. Employees must see safety as a part of their professionalism. A master craftsperson understands the hazards associated with the work they are doing and how to do the work without risk of injury or exposure to danger.

Hierarchy of Hazard Control

When a hazard is identified, there is a hierarchy of control measures OSHA outlines. This states the best solutions down to the least effective.

- **Elimination** – Eliminate the identified hazard altogether. For instance, if a worker must work on something at an elevated level, creating a fall hazard, lower the object to ground level.

- **Substitution** – Replace equipment with safer equipment. Look for a safe alternative; substitute lead paint with non-lead paint…

- **Engineering** – use engineering to isolate the hazard. Creating guards and shielding is an example of engineering controls. Sound proofing to reduce noise is another example…

- **Administration** – Creating a safety policy, standard work instructions and safe work practices.

- **Personal protective equipment** – Wearing ear plugs to protect against loud noises, cut resistant gloves around laceration hazards…

This system is used to eliminate or minimize the identified hazard.

The Safety Performance Cycle: Success Made Simple

At the heart of a safety program is a pattern that is easy to understand and build on.

There is genius in simplicity. The safety performance cycle is simple to understand and yet it's one of the most powerful concepts I know for building an effective and lasting safety program.

The effectiveness of any safety program rests on the ability of those in the organization to recognize and address safety issues on a continuous basis. The safety performance cycle equips employees to do just that.

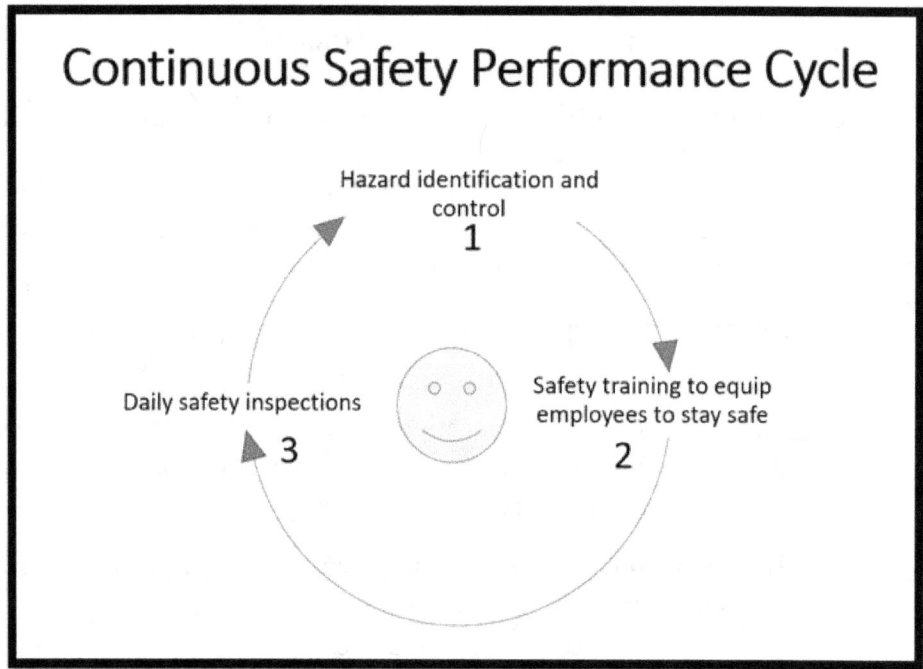

Continuous Safety Performance Cycle

Hazard identification and control
1

Safety training to equip employees to stay safe
2

Daily safety inspections
3

There are five components of a safety management system:
1. **Hazard identification and control**

2. **Safety training**

3. **Safety inspections**

4. Incident investigations

5. Documentation and reporting

This is the starting point and foundation of safety.

Notice that the first three components build on each other. These are the steps of the safety performance cycle. The first three are proactive and the last two are reactive.

It is a continuous process made up of the following:

1. **Capture all hazards/risks** connected with activities, tools, equipment, and the work environment and mitigate risks with control measures. Make sure these are all documented on up-to-date Hazard Identification Risk Assessments (HIRAs). Continuously update HIRAs based on information provided from the safety performance cycle. These are living documents.

2. **Provide safety training** to cover identified hazards and control measures. Create independent safety programs based on identified hazards, such as hearing conservation, confined spaces, fire protection, and hot work. Safety programs are based on identified hazards.

3. **Schedule daily inspections** to uncover danger and address it. This must be viewed as an important part of the daily work routine. Use information learned and go back to step one.

According to the 80/20 principle, 20% of your efforts will bring about 80% of your results. For safety initiatives, the 20% that will bring about the biggest return is the safety performance cycle.

This is the foundation that will support all other safety efforts. If the safety performance cycle is not in place, all your other safety efforts will be weakened.

Simplicity Enables Success

Simplify your safety program as much as possible to make it easier to understand for those you want to keep safe. The people performing the work should feel confident about workplace safety. Ability breeds confidence and the more they understand safety and take pride in their knowledge of it, the more motivated they will be to apply what they know. After all, success lies not in knowledge itself, but in the application of that knowledge. We need safety practitioners and not safety librarians.

We tend to avoid things that are too complex or difficult to understand. When we lack confidence, it's easy to ignore problems and procrastinate. Unfortunately, safety programs can become quite complex. We scrutinize data such as total recordables, first aid cases and perform trend analyses looking to uncover ways to reduce incidents.

I have been in safety meetings where they seemed to believe safety was driven and controlled by spreadsheets. Nothing could be further from the truth. Safety is about people, not numbers. Behavior will always be the biggest driver of safety and performance. Don't get me wrong, we need the data to understand where to focus efforts to improve safety. Once you understand the trends/data, focus on your safety performance cycle.

Equip Employees to Stay Safe

People are at the center of the safety performance cycle. Success in any initiative, project, or task comes down to the motivation and ability of the individuals involved. A people-focus can be viewed as a sixth element to your safety management system. It is that important.

Most of us are motivated to stay safe – no one wants to get hurt. But our minds are often more focused on accomplishing our work rather than doing it safely. After all, the work is what we're being paid to do.

Because of this, safety must be seamlessly blended into work routines and become habitual.

People take pride in what they know and what they do. No one wants to admit they don't understand something or aren't sure what to do next. When we equip employees with simple safety values they can follow, the information becomes intuitive and easy to apply. Safety becomes a source of pride and professionalism, and this increases all levels of work performance.

According to studies in Europe and the United States, a safety program's financial return on investment (ROI) can increase productivity, improve customer service, reduce turnover, and provide savings thanks to fewer injuries and lower workers' compensation costs. When workers know they are valued and can work safely, their focus can go on performing their work tasks with confidence and pride.

Implementing the Safety Performance Cycle

How would you rate your workplace's use of the three main components that make up the safety performance cycle?

Each is easy to understand and measure. Make this your foundation for safety and focus on developing each component:

1. Regularly update HIRAs (Hazard Identification Risk Assessment).

2. Create safety training programs that cover all identified hazards and safety controls.

3. Daily routines must include safety inspections that are simple, focused, and brief.

When these are in place and integrated as part of the work routine, your safety program will become <u>self-monitoring, self-regulating, and self-correcting</u>. Injuries will go down as worker pride goes up.

There is genius in simplicity, but you don't have to be a genius to look like one. Simply implement the safety performance cycle, watch safety improve alongside performance. Then sit back, smile, and let everyone draw their own conclusions.

Hazard Assessment is Step One

The first step in any safety program is to perform a hazard assessment. You cannot protect employees from hazards that you do not know about.

1. **Categories of hazards. This would include:**
   a. **Environmental Hazards**: Extreme cold or heat, poor weather, loud noise, radiation, etc.
   b. **Physical Hazards**: Risk of injury from slip, trip and falls, caught in, engulfment, lacerations, electrical shocks, etc.
   c. **Chemical Hazards**: Exposure to harmful chemicals. Some may cause health problems that may not be detected until later in life.
   d. **Biological Hazards**: Exposure to dangerous animals, insects, people, plants, microorganisms, etc.
   e. **Ergonomic Hazards**: Work this can cause muscle skeletal disorders.
   f. **Workload Hazards**: Overwork can cause stress, fatigue, violence, anxiety, etc.

2. **Rate the hazards.** The higher the rating, the more important the hazard is addressed with a sense of urgency. Base hazards on three criteria:
   a. **Exposure**: How often are people exposed to an identified hazard? (Examples may include hourly, daily, weekly, monthly, annually, etc.)
   b. **Probability:** What is the likelihood of someone getting hurt by the hazard and associated risk? (High, moderate, unlikely).
   c. **Severity**: What would the severity level be if someone did get hurt? Would it be minor such as needing a bandage, or could the injury be fatal? Are multiple deaths possible?

3. **Assign control measures to each hazard** (This removes the danger.)
   a. Follow the OSHA hierarchy of control measures. Get help from experts as needed.
   b. Change the hazard score rating based on effectiveness of the control measures. The new rating shows residual risks that may still need to be addressed.

We created a simple hazard assessment form and used the same template throughout the factory. You can find many types of hazard assessment forms online. A form will help tremendously. Philips/Signify later created a hazard assessment form we used in all operations, and not just manufacturing.

Most hazard assessment forms are designed to rate each identified hazard by probability, severity and level of exposure. You can address the items that pose the greatest dangers first.

The only exception being low hanging fruit, if something can be done immediately to control the identified hazard, do it now! We made these assessments into living documents that were continuously reviewed and updated. These were printed and posted in the work areas and used by our self-directed work teams for training. Anytime someone transferred to a new area, or we received a new employee, they were trained using the hazard assessment.

CHAPTER 5

Behavior-Based Safety

Some people cringe at the sound of those three words. The term "behavior-based safety" gets a bum rap due to misuse. It is often used to place blame on the worker, under the assumption that they must have performed an unsafe act, or they would not have gotten hurt in the first place. Their behavior caused the accident. But we must understand why the employee behaved the way she/he did.

Employees want to succeed at work, and if they get hurt trying to achieve management's set goals, they should not be punished for it. They did not want to get hurt. We need to understand the context of why the employee acted the way they did. (Are they sleep deprived, sick, stressed, overworked, etc.)

I once had a colleague who was the safety manager for a factory in a large city. He swore that he had a few accidents in which employees injured themselves on purpose to collect a settlement. I guess it could happen, but I have never seen this myself.

A work culture is made up of the values and beliefs of those in the work environment. If workers believe that production numbers are valued over safety, they will act accordingly. If they know that their safety and well-being come first, they will set high standards for themselves and others regarding unsafe conditions and behaviors. This is the heart of behavior-based safety.

I highly recommend a safety video called, "Leading Indicators: It's the Little Things," with Jeff "Odie" Espenship. In the video, he outlines three indicators that lead to accidents–

1. Shortcuts

2. Snap decisions

3. Complacency

You can find this video on the American Training Resources web site. You can also find lots of other great safety videos there.

We played this video for everyone at Phillips as part of our annual safety training. We promoted the three leading indicators heavily in our factory, listing them in handouts, safety newsletters, and other venues.

We even had small wallet cards printed with our five-fold approach to safety. To the three leading indicators, we added unsafe acts and unsafe conditions. This became our safety formula for behavior-based safety, to direct employee focus.

You can't control or stop accidents from occurring by a direct approach. This is because no one gets hurt on purpose. We must control accidents indirectly. If there were a dial, we could turn to shut off having accidents, we would have turned it years ago.

Since workers do not generally get hurt on purpose and accidents are trailing indicators of safety, we needed leading indicators to focus on. By making employees aware of the three leading indicators, we gave them something they could watch out for and control.

The core of our behavior-based safety program was defined by these five activities. We called this our **fivefold safety formula**:

1. **Shortcuts:** Watch for and avoid taking shortcuts.

2. **Snap Decisions:** Watch for and avoid making snap decisions (stop and think before acting).

3. **Complacency:** Watch for and avoid complacency about safety. Constantly promote safety.

4. **Unsafe Behavior:** Actively watching out for unsafe behaviors at work as part of daily routine. We are our sisters and brothers' keepers. We protect our team.

5. **Unsafe Conditions:** Actively search out unsafe conditions as part of daily work and create control measures. Allow time daily for safety inspections in work areas. This takes very little time. Use 5S+1. The desired behavior here is to make safety proactive and part of daily routine.

Our safety program was based on these five items and our safety-first culture was continually backed and reinforced by management.

We need to change everyone's mindset about safety, including all management and people in leadership roles.

How do we undo our forty-one years of bad safety habits?

Safety and the Broken Window Theory

The broken window theory was introduced in 1982 by social scientists James Q. Wilson and George L. Kelling. Since the theory was published, it has influenced law enforcement and how we view crime.

The broken window theory: Picture a vacant building with a few broken windows; if not repaired, more will most likely be broken by vandals. With time, the situation will worsen as more vandalism takes place with increased frequency.

What does the broken window theory have to do with safety? It establishes acceptable behavior.

The broken window theory is about normalized behavior and what is considered acceptable.

Safety Rules Not Enforced
Our "Broken Window" Problem

In 2009, our factory was experiencing an alarming rate of accidents. It was also observed that safety rules were not enforced as they should have been. For example, due to noise on the factory floor that exceeded 90+ decibels, hearing protection in the form of ear plugs or muffs was required but rarely used.

Even though everyone knew this, few followed the rule. I observed that few managers, supervisors or anyone in leadership roles wore hearing protection while on the factory floor. This was our broken window.

For years, we have tried to improve our safety without success. We needed to enforce all safety rules, or we could not enforce any of them.

It was not uncommon for employees in this factory to ignore safety rules. It was normal for management to ignore safety rules as well. Safety was not as important as production. Working on equipment while it was running or with guards off was normal. PPE was often not used, Lock Out Tag Out was neglected, the list went on and on.

No one gets hurt on purpose, however in our factory, the control measures needed to keep people safe were not being used. The result was a high number of accidents taking place on a consistent basis. We had the highest accident rate of all our factories globally.

In a brainstorming session with upper management, we talked about our safety problem and how to turn it around, I explained the broken window theory. We needed to start enforcing all safety rules and elevate safety to number one in importance.

New York Crime

In New York city, the crime rate was so bad citizens were removing the stereos to their own cars and placing stickers in the window saying, "No Stereo." This was to keep vandals from breaking a car window to steal the stereo.

City leadership had police officers start enforcing minor law violations.

1. Writing tickets to anyone that jumped a subway turnstile.

2. Writing tickets for "Jaywalking" to panhandlers that were using newspaper to try to wash people's car windows at stoplights.

This set off a chain of improvements in law enforcement. The violent crime rate dropped by 56 percent during the following eight years. Murder, down nearly two-thirds. Robbery, down 67 percent. Aggravated assault, down 28 percent.

Universal Law

There is a universal law that we all follow regarding our behavior. We know what is acceptable and we base our behavior accordingly. We observe what is important to management and adhere to their set values. If safety is not valued by them, it will not be valued by the workforce.

Safety requires effort. If it is not valued, the effort will not be made. Each time a safety rule is broken and not enforced; it sends a message that safety is not important. By not enforcing minor safety violations, we create a culture that does not value safety. The control measures designed to keep employees safe can be disregarded and danger exists where there should be none.

Managers need to make sure that all safety rules are enforced at all levels.

Lesson for Safety

The lesson here is one of acceptable behavior. Safety must be seen as important enough to enforce all safety rules. It takes effort to enforce safety rules, just as it takes effort to stay safe. This effort must begin with management and trickle down through the organization. Managers must be role models for acceptable behavior.

In 2009, we began enforcing all safety rules in our factory. We made sure everyone on the factory floor wore hearing protection. High-level managers walking across the floor made sure they wore ear plugs. They set a good example.

We started the practice of beginning all meetings with safety as the first agenda topic. (This is a practice they still follow today in all Philips/Signify operations). It does not matter what the meeting is for or what department. I regularly audited meetings, and the first topic discussed was our safety stats and any relevant safety news.

Our factory went from being the worse site for safety globally to being one of the best. We received a Philips global safety award in 2011. This made all employees feel proud. It was a great accomplishment.

What is considered acceptable safety behavior where you work? Do you enforce all safety rules? Most safety management systems such as OSAS 18001 and OSHA programs require employers to verify that they are enforcing safety rules.

I have found that it is much more rewarding to place effort into enforcing safety rules than on performing accident investigations. It will be one or the other. Take care of your broken windows and set the acceptable behavior needed for safety. Use leading indicators for driving safety as opposed to lagging indicators.

The First Step: Brainstorm

He said something about wanting to "Think outside the bowel."

Any project, be it personal or professional, begins with a clear understanding of the current condition. We have collected lots of good information over the years that captured all our attempts to improve safety. We had our accident data, and we knew just where we stood in terms of safety for our site. We were not doing well regarding safety and our data verified this.

Admitting the problem is always the first step and we did this. We admitted that we did not know how to improve safety in our factory, or we would have addressed it long ago. Anything we had ever tried to improve safety had failed. This meant years of failure, which is not much of a confidence builder.

Our factory was over forty years old, and our high injury rate had become the norm. The plant manager set up a brainstorming meeting to discuss the problem and possible solutions.

The brainstorming session included the plant manager, his staff, HR, and a few other salary individuals including me. My experience with brainstorming sessions is that it will be good or bad, with no in-betweens. You either come out of it with lots of gold nuggets or you lose a few hours of your life that you will never get back.

This session was golden. None of us were safety experts, but we were committed to turning things around. Our desire to make our factory safe was important and personal for all of us. Our friends were getting hurt, and we wanted to stop this cycle.

Some of the gems we came up with during the brainstorming session included:

- Safety would be our first key performance indicator (KPI). Our KPI's were:

    - Safety

    - Quality

    - Delivery

    - Cost

- We would trade the monthly safety meeting attended mainly by salaried staff for voluntary weekly meetings with the hourly employees.

- We would ask for the hourly employees' help in driving safety and train them to be "dragon slayers."

- We would actively seek out unsafe conditions and behaviors and address them (also done by the hourly workers). Perform hazard assessments in an ongoing manner.

- We would have three safety boards fixed with red, yellow, and green lights. These looked like traffic lights, with one of them being an actual full-size traffic light. If there were no injuries for that day, they stayed green. For a minor injury, they would go yellow, and an OSHA-recordable event that needed outside medical attention would be red. These visual score boards let everyone know if an accident occurred.

- To reward our efforts and successes, any month with no OSHA-recordable injuries was celebrated with steak dinners cooked on site. (That's right…steak dinners; management figured fewer accidents would easily pay for the dinners.)

- We would use the broken window theory and enforce all safety rules.

Beginning in 2009, all meetings began with safety as the first agenda item. This went for every meeting at all levels. Even staff-level meetings began with safety. When I left the factory in 2014, they were still doing this.

These are just a few of the ideas that we implemented from that brainstorming session. Many more ideas, some of which I'll mention later, came directly from the hourly workers. This resulted from their participation in the weekly safety meetings and from working with their co-workers. We kicked off our new "Safety First" program in the beginning of 2009.

CHAPTER 6

Our Safety Journey Begins

We created a core safety team and a safety roadmap. We needed a plan and a blueprint. This helped us implement all the ideas identified in the brainstorming session.

The core safety team consisted of the production manager, human resources, a few key department heads, and me. We meet once a month to review the safety road map and make sure we implemented all that we had said we would. The safety road map identified projects and improvements, progress, owners and completion dates.

We reviewed the effectiveness of our efforts and adjusted as needed. Having a roadmap gave us a sense of urgency and clarity. Each month, we assigned items that would be reviewed the following month. Some of these items were quite small, but they kept us moving forward. Progress is important. Improving safety is like following a guiding star and not a distant shore. This is a process of continuous improvement.

As we moved forward with all the activities on our safety roadmap, we followed the PDCA cycle (Plan Do Check Act). If something was not giving us the desired results, we would tweak it or drop it for something that worked better.

We typically close the factory from Christmas through New Year's Day each year. When everyone returned to work at the start of 2009, each employee was hand-delivered a safety memo written by our plant manager. It laid out our new safety commitment. The plant manager made it clear that he cared about our employees' safety.

This first step was met with disbelief. We had always had a "production numbers come first" culture (Performance Culture) and this change was going to be a tough sell. Employees would have to see a real change in management's values before they embrace this new plan. Based on their experience, they did not believe safety could ever be put ahead of production.

We immediately started implementing the decisions made in the brainstorming session. HR publicized the new safety meeting structure; we would meet weekly, before or after shifts. The meetings would be sixty minutes long. They would be voluntary, and employees that attended them would be paid for their time. We found with time that we only needed thirty minutes to conduct the meeting.

Our Safety Meeting Structure:
- The Core Safety Team meets once per month.
- Safety Team: Included all employees and a meeting was held every week. Meetings alternated in times to take place before or after a shift. Employees were paid to attend, and attendance was voluntary.

Sixty minutes of extra pay for simply attending a meeting was easy to go along with, even with the already-long hours. We knew they were motivated by the money, but we also thought we could engage them in helping over the course of time. As I stated before, we found that thirty-minute meetings worked best for us.

These meetings were crucial for our safety transformation. Had it not been for the support and engagement of the hourly employees, our renewed safety initiative would have failed as dismal as those we had tried in the past.

For a safety program to be successful, it must have full management support, employee buy-in and engagement. I have visited different operations and facilities where I have been asked how they can improve safety. I always say it begins with management commitment to put safety first. (Then train all employees to be dragon slayers.) Follow the safety performance cycle.

Does this mean you must have weekly safety meetings? Not at all. We wanted to engage employees as quickly as possible, and we used the meetings to build momentum and improve communication.

It's important that communication between all levels of workers is open and consistent while giving everyone the chance to talk and voice concerns and suggestions. Our meetings did this. Find what works for you. You need a good structure for open communication.

Changing the culture of any organization is not easy and it will not happen overnight. We knew we would have to invest a lot of time and energy. For a commercial jet to take off, it needs far more thrust than is needed to maintain level flight. In the same manner, we needed to give massive effort to the "take off" of our new safety initiative.

We needed a MAP, a Massive Action Plan, and that is what we had. We launched our own internal awareness campaign to promote our new Safety-First program. We put a lot of "thrust' into our new safety program takeoff.

All employees know what is important to management. For us, it was always "production numbers first," going for high product yield and low scrap, low equipment down time. Our work culture had always been performance driven and this was reinforced continually.

In studies performed in manufacturing environments on morale, the main factor determining worker satisfaction and good morale was consistently hitting set targets. We tend to be competitive by nature, and all of us want to succeed. If a production line in a factory has a target of running at 95% efficiency and it is running at 96%, workers are happy, life is good, and morale is high. If that same production line is running 80% on another day, morale is low as mechanics fight to get back to the desired efficiency target.

This was an important factor for us to recognize, because this was what we had to address. How could we achieve balance? We needed the numbers, but not at the expense of worker safety. All businesses will deal with this aspect of safety VS performance. We must help employees be successful at both.

All our employees understood the reality of business. With a high-speed production line making fluorescent lamps, a high percentage of scrap could mean the difference between profit and loss. We knew we had to hit production targets, but not by putting workers at risk. Would you put an adult son or daughter at risk of injury for profit?

People Must Come First before Safety Can Come First

(This is Leadership)

A company I have always admired for its commitment to people and safety is Proctor and Gamble. Their values state: "P&G is its people and the values by which we live. . . . We act on the conviction that our men and women will always be our most important asset."

Statements such as this set up a culture of caring for one another. This is where safety begins: People must come first before safety can come first. Without that commitment, there is no need for a safety-first culture because employees are viewed as simply a means to an end. They are an expendable commodity, and safety is not in the picture.

When employees are cared for, respected, and empowered, it's like electricity hitting a light bulb. The environment comes to life. Morale goes up as employees engage. The workforce becomes a dynamic, learning organization in which the whole is greater than the sum of its parts or individuals.

Like a family, all employees must be valued as important. "You are one of us and we look out for each other." This is establishing a community at work. One way to encourage this is by creating a team atmosphere, with everyone identifying themselves as part of a team. The team could be a department, a production line, or whatever unit makes sense in your work environment. Teams foster relationships as we look out for those on our team.

If your business is too small for teams, simply make one team. Your perspective for employee safety should be, "You work for us, and we look out for each other. Your safety comes first. I will look out for you and please look out for me."

If you look at work from a community perspective, you look for what is best for everyone in the community. If management's decisions are not good for everyone, they are not good for anyone. You don't rob Peter to pay Paul. "All for one and one for all" is a great safety moto. Everyone matters, or it will seem like no one matters. The three musketeers had it right!

Management must not have an attitude of entitlement that puts their desire for a bonus or promotion over employee safety. Employees will not trust anyone that acts as if they are better than those they manage. Honestly . . . do you? If someone can make decisions that affect my work conditions and they are basing their decisions on what is best for themselves alone, conflicts will arise.

Here is some food for thought: If a company puts profit ahead of employees, they will most likely put profit ahead of customers and suppliers as well. My advice is not to associate with those companies.

Would you eat at a restaurant that openly stated they valued profit over customer satisfaction? Would you use a doctor if he told you he only became a doctor to make lots of money.

Profit is the result of good business. When a company provides quality products or services and control cost, they profit. We want them to profit so they can continue to provide the products or services needed to us. Once profit becomes the main goal, however, products and services will suffer.

The successful business model puts people first. Employees are people, customers are people, and suppliers are people. If management is willing to exploit one of these, they will most likely exploit all of them. Employees, customers and suppliers are in a symbiotic relationship. Any decision that hurts one of them hurts the business. Bad decisions harm all of them. We want the win/win/win by basing decisions on what is best for all three groups. Good business decisions benefit employees, customers and suppliers. This is what makes a sustainable business.

To survive as a civilization, people must have a sense of community. It is about collaboration, working together, finding a need and meeting the need. Only through collaboration does the whole become greater than the sum of its individual parts, in this case, individual people. We will always accomplish more as a group than on our own.

To achieve community, management must see the bigger picture and put selfishness aside. This is about good leadership. A good leader will never sacrifice what is yours to protect what is his but will willingly sacrifice what is his to protect what is yours.

I love the scene in the movie "The 300," when King Leonidas of the Spartans and King Xerxes of the invading Persian army are talking. King Xerxes says, "There is not one of my men I would not gladly sacrifice for victory." King Leonidas responds, "And there is not one of my men that I would not willingly die for." That's leadership.

We need more good leaders in our businesses and in our government. Good leaders are rare, and they stand out.

Face to Face Safety

In 2003 I was the supervisor for a large department in our factory that ran 24/7, I was used to long hours. I remember arriving at work early one morning to find my boss walking into our offices off the factory floor. I was worried that something bad had happened. When I asked if everything was ok, he told me yes, I was just out visiting with workers about safety. My manager and mentor explained that he wanted employees to know safety is important to management. He conveyed to them that he never wants safety risks taken for driving performance. Performance must be sustainable, which requires employee engagement and safety.

He also loved pointing out; we are social beings. It is human nature to talk about what's important to us. When managers, supervisors or anyone in a leadership role do not engage in face-to-face safety talks, the message workers pick up on is; Safety is not important.

Safety Begins with Role Models

People in authority positions must be role models for safety. This is where safety begins. As employees work for any organization, they should receive a consistent message about the importance of safety. At the Philips factory, where I was the safety officer and senior trainer, we integrated safety into all we did. People in leadership positions were expected to be safety role models.

Examples of our talking safety reinforcement:

- The new Higher employee orientation began with explaining our "Safety-First" culture and our commitment to employee safety. Safety training took up the largest portion of the new hire orientation. Their first day was eight hours of safety training.

- ALL meetings in our factory began with safety as the first agenda item. It did not matter what level or department; ALL meetings began by reviewing our safety efforts and progress. (I regularly audited meetings to verify this.)

- All training, performance appraisals, and projects began with safety reviews and talks.

- Time was scheduled for supervisors, managers, etc., to go to the shop floor and perform face-to-face safety talks.

The Gallup organization and other pole groups have questioned employees about how they receive information at work and what their preference is for communication. Face-to-face is always the number one answer.

Employees know management only invests time in what's important. If their immediate boss does not regularly set aside time to talk about safety, the perception received is safety does not matter.

Health and Safety Management System

A health and safety management system can be defined as all the activities and the structure used to manage safety. I will outline a Health and Safety Management System later in this book. Communication of safety rules, initiatives, goals, and status is an important piece of the EHSM system. Create a structured approach for your work safety communication that includes scheduled face time dedicated wholly to safety.

The time invested will be returned many folds as communication uncovers opportunities. Scheduled safety talks, one on one or in groups, are a leading indicator of proactive safety. Capture how often safety is talked about formally and use it as a safety metric. I have witnessed in many locations that when safety talks go up, accidents and near misses go down.

We need leading indicators we can focus on to drive all safety efforts. Frequency and positive reception of safety talks is a good leading indicator of a healthy work safety culture. Record your safety talks and their outcomes. Capture reception level, (good or bad), topics discussed, safety dilemmas, concerns, etc.

Effective Communication and Influence

Employers that choose memos, email and bulletin boards as their main forms of safety communication are choosing efficiency over effectiveness. The best forms of communication regarding effectiveness, in order, are:
1. Face to face
2. Video chat
3. Phone
4. Texting
5. Email

We need a two-way dialogue. This is proactive communication. Questions can be asked and answered. We want loyalty and trust connected to all work-related activities, including safety. Our strongest ability to influence is face to face with kindness and caring. Even our body chemistry verifies this. Flesh and bone communication like this release's oxytocin and serotonin. These hormones connect us and build our sense of trust and loyalty.

How effective is your safety communication? Are you making the most of safety leading indicators or are you relying primarily on lagging indicators such as incidents and near misses?

If you're not scheduling safety face time with employees, here is a great opportunity for you to improve safety. Make face-to-face safety talks, one of your leading indicators for driving safety. Watch your incidents go down as your employee loyalty and trust go up.

CHAPTER 7

No One Wants to Get Hurt

As a safety professional, I've performed hundreds of accident investigations. Never have I heard an injured person say, "I knew I was going to get hurt if I did that." As stated earlier, we take risks for many reasons, and depending on the culture of the shop floor, the risks taken may become the norm.

When workers know a task is dangerous, they try to be careful, but it comes down to the law of averages. If enough risks are taken often enough, at some point injuries will occur. Workers should not be exposed to danger as part of their employment. When people come to work, they are paid to perform work tasks. They have no desire to get injured performing those tasks.

To make matters worse, when an employee gets hurt performing a dangerous task assigned to him or her, management will most likely blame the injured employee for getting hurt.

Most employees want to succeed at their jobs. There are many motivators to succeed, such as job security, financial security, pride, and self-esteem. We want to avoid injuries, but we will take risks, if necessary, to succeed at our work.

Whenever an employee is hurt at work, management must take responsibility. After all, the worker was simply trying to get work done. There is often more motivation to succeed at a task than to perform it in a safe fashion.

Since employers are responsible for the tasks employees perform, it is up to management to take a proactive stance on workplace safety. This means actively flushing out unsafe conditions and unsafe acts. It is up to the employer to provide a safe work environment. This includes making sure safety rules are understood and enforced.

Safety rules must be enforced, and employee reprimands are necessary for breaking safety rules. But we do the employee a great injustice if we do not look at the full context of "why" the employee did not follow the rules. Other employees may be acting the same way regarding safety. Remember the "Broken Window Theory."

Chain of Events

When doing accident investigations, I often find that what leads to the injury was a chain of events. What I mean by chain of events is there are often many factors that lead up to the accident.

For example, we had some areas of our factory that had wet floors due to the lamp paint process. Paint would spill on the floor and water was constantly used to remove it. Employees that worked in the area knew the floor could provide a slip hazard, so they were careful.

If an employee slipped and fell on the wet floor, it would typically involve a chain of events such as this; a worker is working on equipment in the area, an alarm goes off on a nearby production line signaling a problem, they have tools in their hands and rush to shut off the alarm, slipping on the wet floor.

If they are just walking from point A to point B, they know how to be careful, but workers multi-task and what is typically not much of a problem or danger becomes one.

Another example - employees know not to stick their hands in moving parts of running equipment. A chain of events may include a guard being removed to observe equipment running to diagnose a problem before shutting the equipment down, A tool falls into the equipment such as a flashlight and the mechanic instinctively reacts and reaches for the tool, the moving equipment meets a hand, and you have an injury.

There is typically more than one factor leading to an accident. These can include fatigue, multitasking, snap decisions, shortcuts, complacency, lack of training and rushing. Look for the different scenarios that can lead to an accident and work to address these in advance. Uncover and document the full context in your investigation.

Management must not just blame the workers for getting hurt. Spend more time and energy flushing out unsafe conditions and acts. For unsafe acts, we want to ask **why** the employee broke safety rules? Did they feel pressured, etc.?

Safe, By Accident
(Also called being Lucky)

How is your worker safety program doing? If you're not having any incidents (injuries, near misses and property damage.), do you know why? To what do you attribute your success? Do you have a robust safety culture and safety management system that is proactively promoting safety or are you being safe by accident, just being lucky? The problem with luck is, it runs out.

We can't sustain success unless we understand WHY we are successful. We do incident investigations when things go wrong, but how about when they go right? Success leaves clues: we need to pay attention to them and understand today's safety success and leverage it for tomorrow's safety success.

Remember, the way we shifted out of learned helplessness regarding safety was by studying employees that were already successful at working safely. We learned that we could control safety. It was within our power to eliminate injuries. We could improve employee confidence regarding safety and build their self-esteem. Master craftsmen understand safety as part of their work and professionalism. We wanted our employees to see themselves as master craftsmen.

Creating a Safety Culture

What mechanisms must be in place for improving safety and reducing incidents? Here is what you need to know to implement a successful safety culture at work.

1. **Management Commitment. Create a formal Safety Policy:** Management must commit to keeping workers safe. The best practice for safety is to create a formal safety policy and post it for all to see. Safety first means people come first. This is how management shows they value employees. Without management commitment, your safety efforts will fizzle before it begins. Employees that don't feel valued are more likely to take risks to protect their jobs.

2. **Employee Commitment:** Employees need to believe they can work accident-free and agree to strive for zero accidents as the goal. They must commit to putting safety first. This is a commitment to be proactive in protecting themselves and coworkers. Employees know performance is important and will do their best to make the business successful. We want them to do this in a safe way. You want employees to feel valued.

3. **Safety Training:** Employees must be taught about the hazards they could be exposed to and the control measures created to keep them safe. Training must be viewed as important and continuous. Training is how we equip employees to stay safe at work. Employees must see safety as an aspect of performance and professional development. Master craftswomen and craftsmen understand safety's importance.

4. **Proactive safety activities**: Mechanisms for driving safety must include a way for employees to flush out and address unsafe conditions and behaviors. This includes such activities as 5S+1, daily safety audits, safety meetings, safety talks, inspections and hazard assessments. These activities are leading indicators which can be measured. Leading indicators drive the lagging indicators.

5. **Communication Systems for safety**: Management needs to use every available opportunity to promote safety. We made safety the first agenda item for ALL meetings in our facility. Safety was promoted on team boards, safety walks and with newsletters. Employees had a system for reporting unsafe conditions and behaviors. Utilize face to face safety talks.

6. **Safety Celebrations and Rewards**: Employees want positive management recognition. They know that management celebrates important events and goals. No rewards and recognition for safety means it's not important. Look for ways to celebrate safety often.

7. **Good record keeping and analysis of all incidents**: Incident investigations need to be thorough, timely and include root cause analysis. We must recognize trends and understand the cause. Make good record keeping a part of all health and safety management efforts. Audit your safety record keeping annually. This will be a big help if you ever have an OSHA inspection.

Proactive Safety

Safety is proactive, or it's inactive. Your safety initiatives need to be continuously monitored and promoted. These activities serve as leading indicators towards safety success. When you see effort diminish towards any of the above-listed programs, you can bet incidents will rise. These are the mechanisms for driving safety. Your leading indicators will drive your lagging indicators.

We love "wins," at work and in life, make safety one of them. I would rather spend time promoting safety than doing accident investigations. Build on the safety momentum you get by thanking employees for working safely and reinforcing that this is no accident. (No pun intended.) They are safe by following safe work habits. Reward their safety success!

We never want to be simply "safe by accident; lucky." Analyze why you're having safety success and leverage it. Employee and management confidence will grow as they uncover the correlation between safety efforts and outcomes. You are creating an upward spiral by recognizing and building on safety successes.

Push vs. Pull

Understanding push vs. pull is important when driving any new initiative, whether it is safety, continuous improvement, or performance. Most of us, when pushed, push back. This disengages employees and gets employers the bare minimum return from employee effort.

We are emotional beings, and short-term decisions are often based on emotions, feelings, and impulses. It would be nice to think that we based our decisions on reason and logic, but we often act from emotions, feelings or impulses and use reason and logic later to validate our actions.

The Gallup Poll tracks employee engagement and noted that in 2014, only one-third of U.S. workers were engaged in their jobs. "According to a November 2023 Gallup poll, 33% of U.S. employees are engaged, and 17% are actively disengaged. This is higher than the 26% of employees that were engaged when Gallup started measuring in 2000, but lower than the 36% in 2020. Globally, 23% of employees are engaged, but best-practice organizations have **70% engaged employees.**" – Gallup

Employees in manufacturing and production jobs recorded the lowest levels of engagement, with an average of 23%. As I mentioned before, manufacturing environments can be dehumanizing and flat out depressing. I have visited factories in the U.S., China, Mexico, and Canada, and I have observed many amazing workers in challenging work environments.

It's encouraging that most of the management teams I have had the chance to visit are caring people that want to improve working conditions. Their efforts were often trial and error, as they faced many obstacles and constraints. Operation budgets are squeezed to boost shareholder dividends. Those that perform the work can suffer from lack of funding for any programs that improve employee satisfaction and safety.

Layers of bureaucracy, red tape, and constant changes in management often contribute to the challenge of improving safety and working conditions. This is another reason why safety programs need to be clearly structured, communicated and have a safety policy in place. The safety program needs to be robust and well-structured to survive in a complex multi-level corporate environment. If worker safety initiatives and programs are not continuously promoted, they can slide down in importance overshadowed by performance and profit.

Affective managers realize that there are great opportunities for future business success resting in the untapped potential of disengaged employees. It goes back to fostering an attitude of community at work.

Employees want to succeed and help the company hit its goals. For them, this means steady work, income, and pride. But rather than involve employees via clear goals and training, management usually tries to push decisions down from above and employees disengage and push back.

We need more "pull" and less "push". Pull is when employees are motivated and willing to use their own creativity and energy to solve work-related problems. In the pull environment, employees feel valued and respected. They feel like stakeholders and want to contribute to the success of the business. They feel valued.

We want employees to understand important business goals and how they can contribute. You need to help them succeed so they can help you succeed.

If the workers are coming up with ideas, solutions, and projects, they are engaged. Most people do not like being told what to do (push); they would rather be told what the problem is and given the opportunity to come up with their own solutions (pull).

Just as management must be 100% in support of safety with no double talk or BS, the shop floor must be fully committed to putting safety first. If management is not behind it 100%, it will most likely fail. You cannot have the management team using a public voice that says, "Safety First," and a shop floor voice that says, "Do whatever it takes."

Once management makes the commitment that all employees put safety first, employees will test management's commitment. They will surface performance VS safety dilemmas.

Any time there is a conflict between doing something safe versus allowing an employee to risk injury to protect efficiency numbers, safety must win. These situations may always have existed, but now employees will drag them into the light to be addressed.

If dangerous work is done on running equipment, workers will need to shut down the equipment to perform repairs and adjustments. Since some adjustments may require the equipment to be running, safe ways must be found to perform these tasks.

Remember the moral safety compass test: Would you let an adult son or daughter perform the task? If not, don't let anyone else do it, either.

The numbers may suffer at first, but this will quickly turn around. When employees are valued and morale is high, they will come up with more ideas to drive improvement than any management team ever could have. I have witnessed this in many different work environments.

It is important that the people doing the work be involved in all changes made for the sake of their own safety. After all, they are the ones that could get hurt.

When a hazard is identified there is often a control measure that must be implemented as stated by your governing safety administration such as OSHA. The workers are the ones that will find ways around safety control measures if they do not agree with them, or if they make work too difficult. The workers must live with all the changes made for the sake of safety. If the changes impede their ability to do the work or make the work more difficult, they will navigate around safety controls to get the job done. This is conservation of energy at work.

We do not want employees to ignore safety controls or create OSHA violations. We need them to have a basic knowledge of workplace safety. Employees must understand basic safety protocols. Knowledge is power and, in this case, it is the power to keep workers safe.

CHAPTER 8

Equip, Empower, and Support

Step one is to train all employees in safety. Government agencies in many countries are encouraging (or demanding) that an outlined health and safety management system be in place. OSHA compliance in the U.S., OSHA International, NEBOSH, and systems such as OSAS 18001 ensure that there is a structured approach to worker health and safety.

Many of our Philips/Signify facilities were OSAS 18001 certified and worked hard to ensure OSHA compliance. Our facility in San Marcos TX, was an OSHA VPP STAR certified site. It was certified in 2011 and is still certified as of 2023. The OSHA VPP STAR certification requires a strong commitment to safety by management and strong active engagement by employees. The program is a good example of what can be achieved through training, empowerment and support.

Training employees in safety practices and hazard awareness is an important component of the health and safety management system. Let's face it, for any activity in life, training is the first step. You cannot neglect training in potential work hazards and the control measures that ensure safety.

Agencies such as OSHA require that all employees be trained in many safety topics, such as personal protective equipment, hearing conservation, fall protection, emergency response, and so forth. Safety training topics are based on identified hazards. It is up to the employer to make sure they are covering all the required safety training topics as well as compliance with all other government safety agency rules.

Employers should not try to avoid compliance but rather work with these agencies. This will go a long way in case of an audit or an employee complaint. If a representative of the agency is already working with you, they will see you as a company that cares about worker safety and is trying to do the right thing for employees. This will help you not only with safety, but with avoiding penalties for non-compliance.

For any recognized hazard that exists in a work environment, there must be control measures in place and employees must be trained and competent in using the control measures.

Employers can obtain a list of all required safety training topics. This can often be obtained from websites of agencies such as OSHA, OH&S (in Canada), and OSHA International. You can also obtain lists of training needed from many of the health and safety products and service vendors. Any of them that provide safety training for compliance can tell you what is required. Websites such as safeopedia.com are another great resource for information and networking.

Once an employer understands all required training and who must take it, they will need to make sure they comply by scheduling the training needed and keeping records of its effectiveness. For some training, evidence of passing a test may be needed to validate the training effectiveness. At the very least, you will need to record:

- Date of training

- Training topics

- Names of the trainers

- A copy of the training material presented.

- A list of trainees that includes their signatures to verify attendance

Once employees understand the hazards they can be exposed to, and the safety controls in place to protect them, they can keep an eye out for work hazards as a part of their standard work. Risk assessments are an important component of an affective health and safety management system. Hazards can be created quickly, and employees must be trained in how to identify and address them.

Schedule Safety walks to identify hazards and record what you find. This validates that you are taking a consistent, structured approach to identifying hazards. If your company is implementing Lean Manufacturing, 5S+1 is a useful tool that can meet this requirement. I will discuss it in detail later in this book.

As part of job orientation, employees must be trained in all hazards they could encounter as part of their work environment and tasks. Job shadowing is the most popular way to train employees. From cooking in a restaurant, to becoming a construction worker, we learn from those that have gone before us.

This is called tribal knowledge--the older, more experienced members of the tribe train the younger or newer ones. The problem with this is the possible lack of consistency and quality.

Just because someone is good at what he or she does will not necessarily mean they will be good at teaching others. In fact, I have met many skilled craftsmen who were horrible trainers. Many of them simply did not like training others.

They would purposely gloss over details and steps to get the training over with. They might tell their trainees, "You will get it with time; don't worry." A better approach is to embrace standard work instructions.

CHAPTER 9

Standard Work Instructions

Implementing standard work can improve safety dramatically. It can also greatly improve quality, and all other aspects derived from a work task. Standard work is the only way to achieve sound training and a capable, reliable, repeatable process. Standard work becomes the blueprint for any task, an instruction guide that can be referred to over and over.

Standard work has two levels, the "What" and the "How."

What - Is a list of all tasks to be performed by a worker. What they will be doing.
How - Is detailed instructions on how to perform each listed task safely and successfully.

Example A: Job Shadowing only –

Let's say I have come to work at your business. Your method of training is to job shadow. I may watch a brief training video or spend some time in orientation, but for the most part, my training comes from the fine individual I am placed with. The only documentation may be recording the amount of time spent with my trainer learning the job.

Example B: Job Shadow + Standard Work –

In this scenario, I come to work for you and as part of my orientation, you use standard work. I am handed a sheet of paper or a booklet that lists all the work tasks I will perform during my shift. This will go a long way toward putting a new employee at ease.

All of us want to know what to expect and what is expected of us. To have a list of all the work tasks I will do during my day lets me know what my average day will consist of before I engage in the activity. I am then able to mentally prepare and engage. I still need to job shadow, but both the trainer and trainee now have a structure to follow. The training will be more effective.

You see how much better Example B is than Example A? With standard work, a new employee will be more relaxed and can ask better questions. There is an identified structure to follow that they can hold on to and absorb.

The "How" is a set of work instructions created for each identified work task. The new employee has a list of all work activities they will engage in during a shift. The next piece of the puzzle is, "How do I perform each of these tasks?"

Work instructions can be created showing in detail how each task is done. This is the safest, most efficient procedure known today for performing each task. When a better method is developed, the standard work instructions are updated.

It does not matter what work is being done. If you work in a restaurant, factory, construction site, hospital, or retail store, our intention is to create processes that are capable, repeatable and reliable. Detailed instructions for each task are the only way to achieve this.

Safety and efficiency go hand in hand. People do not get hurt as often when everything is going right. It is when things go south, and we need to react to the unconventional that injury rates go up. A process mechanic in a factory is not as apt to get hurt when the equipment is running smoothly. The construction worker is safest when the work is on schedule and well organized.

A side benefit to standard work is improved efficiency and quality. Part of the reasons that franchises are so successful is that customers know what to expect from them. Standard work is in place. Standard work removes variation and creates consistency in products and services.

Customers want a certain experience, and franchises deliver it. For example, if I go to a McDonald's in my hometown of Salina, KS or in Dallas, TX, the food and experience will be similar. The restaurants will look the same, the employees will dress the same, and the food will taste the same. This can only be accomplished through standard work.

These businesses have greatly reduced variation. Everything is standardized. They buy supplies from the same vendors, use the same equipment to prepare the food, and follow the same standard work instructions. The result is the same predictable experience, which is capable of meeting customers' requirements. The processes are reliable and repeatable. This is what customers, employers, and employees all want. No surprises.

Standard work instructions set everyone up for success.

After the "what" and the "how" are created for standard work, a standard training process can be created for new employees. That's right, standard work should be created for employee training.

When a person is hired, as part of training, the trainer can use a set training guide and check off each item as the new employee is told about it. Competency can be validated with time as needed. If thirty days is typically the minimum time for learning the required skill, a thirty-day review can be scheduled to measure progress.

When I was the senior trainer for Philips, we used a 30, 60, 90-day review process. I told all employees the purpose of this was to ensure their success. We made it a very positive experience and provided them with more training as needed. We wanted them to succeed!

Another great advantage of standard work is the ability to continually improve it. Standard work becomes a baseline. As employees find better ways to do a job or as new technologies are developed, the standard work instructions are revised.

Standard work instructions should be reviewed and updated annually. In one of my last improvement projects, I worked with a group that used standard work, but the instructions had not changed in over fifteen years! This resulted in a horribly antiquated, ineffective process, and their customers were suffering for it. The employees using the outdated standard work instructions had high frustration levels from it.

Once employees are trained in hazard awareness, safety, and the use of standard work instructions, they need some freedom to drive improvements. As an employer, you have just invested time and money in training employees, so why wouldn't you want them to make use of that training? The people that do the daily work know what problems and safety issues they face. They need some freedom and empowerment to drive improvements. Let them slay the dragons menacing them.

When a problem occurs in a work environment, the employees that perform work in the area daily will most likely identify it first. When a problem is identified, employers will often follow a "Traditional Leader/Follower" approach or an "Empowered Employee" approach.

Choice One: The Traditional Leader/Follower Approach –

In this business model, when problems are identified at the lowest levels, they are reported to management and kicked upstairs to someone with authority to decide on how to deal with it. The problems inherent in this system are numerous.

Management may not care because they are not the ones who feel the pain from the concern that is causing trouble for a lower-level employee.

Since managers have their own plate of work and must meet the expectations of their bosses, they may give little attention to something brought to them by a low-level employee. Constraints with time, money, and other resources may cause them to shelve their concern for a later date. Red tape and a cumbersome system of gaining the go-ahead to act can kill a project at any level as the request sits on a desk or in someone's in-basket.

Choice Two: Empower Employees at All Levels to Drive Small Improvements –

Rather than kick information upstairs to those that are already busy and may not care, let's push some decision-making down to those that see the problems most clearly. In Lean Manufacturing terms, this is called "kaizen," which means "a small improvement for the better." The power of kaizen is that it empowers those that do the work to come up with solutions to identified problems.

I have seen first-hand how incredibly powerful kaizens can be when embraced at all levels. I have also seen what happens when management shows disrespect to the employee by saying they can't make or suggest improvements. They may be told that this is not their job.

If you don't want to use the term "kaizen" don't. Call the program whatever you want. Just implement a way for employees to drive improvements.

You don't want a suggestion box. We want to encourage and help employees come up with small projects they can do themselves. They can make a habit of making improvements.

People are used to making decisions at home. They budget money, manage households, and raise children. If a system for kaizens is put in place, employees will come up with many great ideas for making improvements. It is in our nature to improve work that is important to us.

Of course, the amount of freedom given to an employee will largely depend on the work environment. I can foresee a little more freedom in a machine shop or restaurant, as compared to working in a nuclear power plant.

For control, standard work on implementing kaizen must be created and embraced. This would include some checks and balances. For instance, identified safety projects could require the sign-off of the safety officer or safety manager. This would ensure compliance with safety rules and agencies.

Employees and their supervisors can work together to set and agree on improvements. Getting coworker buy-in is a great litmus test for potential projects. If coworkers disagree with a suggested improvement project, it can be studied further or canceled. The only exceptions would be if it was the only solution identified for a problem that must be addressed regarding safety.

Small improvements can be implemented quickly, and standard work instructions updated as needed.

A simple form can be created to list the desired improvement or kaizen project. It can follow this simple format:

1. What is the identified problem?

2. What solution has been identified to fix it?

3. Who will be responsible for implementing the solution?

4. When will it be done?

A standard form that captures this information can quickly be reviewed by fellow employees, team leaders, department heads, front line supervisors, or anyone else that needs to be involved. When approval is given, the project can move forward. It can also be easily reversed if the desired results do not occur.

It is easy for a manager or department head to review such a form and give a simple yes or no. More information can be requested, and if the answer is "No, we can't do this," a reason needs to be given. If an employee takes the time to fill out the form and wants to drive an improvement, they deserve to know why it can't be done at this time.

Standard work for suggesting and implementing improvements must be created and followed. You are giving employees an avenue for making suggestions and implementing solutions. This is not a suggestion box. That would be falling back to the traditional approach. With kaizen, the employee identifies the problem, suggests the solution, and implements it if he or she is able.

If the idea is sound and the project completed, the employee that suggested the idea should get credit even if a specialist or engineer was involved. We need to encourage engagement and thank employees for going above and beyond.

In our factory in 2009, our employees identified over 500 safety Kaizens. By the end of 2010, we had completed over 1,000! Most of these projects were identified by front-line workers. For more information on standard work, check out my Standard Work Instructions short YouTube video.

CHAPTER 10

Safety Meetings and Safety Boards

When it came to our new safety-first initiative, the hourly employees stepped up and were the real heroes that made it work. I told them that as the safety officer, I felt like an orchestra conductor. I was leading, but they were the ones making the music.

Once the hourly workers accepted that this "safety first thing" was for real and management was supporting it, they came alive with innovative ideas. The weekly safety meetings were helpful for building momentum. (We were employing more thrust for our safety initiative take-off) and keeping everyone's focus on safety.

When we started having the weekly volunteer safety meetings, they were an hour long. In time, we shortened them to thirty minutes. To encourage safety meeting attendance, employees received credits for attending. (They were also paid) This was reflected in their performance reviews and tied to bonuses.

Employees received a small bonus based on their performance review scores. The bonus was not much and did not compare with the overtime paid for just attending the meetings, but it was still money on the table for employees.

We kept the meetings relaxed and informal while still following a set agenda. I started each meeting by showing a funny YouTube video or showing funny safety pictures. This went a long way towards getting people to relax and contribute.

Here is the Safety Meeting Agenda we follow:

- Humerus videos as people got settled
- Review of our safety statistics
  - Accidents
  - Near misses
- Review of any accidents from the previous week
- Review identified safety concerns (These came from anyone in the meeting)
- Review any upcoming safety projects and events.
- Conduct short safety training if needed
- Present one safety highlight such as PPE or LOTO

- Highlight one aspect of health, such as nutrition, sleep, or exercise

Once we enlisted the help of our hourly employees, our safety activities began to accelerate. We asked how we could direct more attention to safety. We wanted a safety awareness campaign.

Here are just a few of the ideas brought to the safety team meetings that we used with good success:

- One person had the idea of creating a safety T-shirt and giving one to each person that turned in a completed safety kaizen project. The T-shirts then became walking reminders for safety. We have done this for years, and on any given day, you could see a good percentage of our employees (hourly and salaried) wearing Safety-First T-shirts. We made a new design each year.

- We set up a safety mascot and would change it each year. Our first was a life-size cardboard cut-out of Superman. Whenever anyone was hurt, we put a Band-Aid on the man of steel, showing what part of the body was hurt. This was a strong visual that got lots of attention. No one liked seeing Band-Aids on Superman. We put him in a high traffic area and even brought him into our safety meetings. Visitors always noticed and commented on our mascot. A bonus to this visual aid was that people were able to see what parts of the body were getting hurt the most. Hand injuries were high as shown by the Band-Aids. This encouraged the wearing of cut resistant gloves.

- Since all hourly employees were on self-directed work teams, the teams presented the latest safety projects done in their areas in the safety meetings, thus giving recognition to the team and its individuals.

- A safety sign was designed by an hourly mechanic that said, STOP – THINK – ACT. These were placed on any equipment or in any area where an accident or near-miss had occurred. These were warnings and reminders that someone had been hurt or was almost hurt there.

The hourly workers registered 545 safety projects in our manufacturing facility in 2009. Of those 545, over 90% were completed, driven by the shop floor employees.

These were just a few of the projects. Remember there were 545, too many to detail here! This had a positive impact on morale. In Town Hall meetings and at every other opportunity, our plant manager reinforced the Safety-First message and thanked employees for their safety efforts.

In the beginning, this was met with some disbelief. With time, it became our culture, and we were still hitting our production targets!

We also had a few strategically placed safety boards that contained relevant health and safety information. We posted safety meeting times and agenda items. We also used the board to brag about safety wins and make announcements. Any safety-related content that we wanted to promote went on the safety boards. We also posted safety cartoons and fun information to encourage looking at the boards.

We created a health and safety calendar for the year. Each month we highlighted one safety topic, such as "lock out tag out," hearing protection, or guards. We also picked one health topic, such as vaccinations, skin cancer, or quitting smoking. For each of these topics, we provided short training and information.

We often had pamphlets that employees could take home. Many free health pamphlets are available from organizations such as the Red Cross and the American Cancer Society.

Safety mascots 2009 – 2012

2009 Safety t-shirt

CHAPTER 11

Great Safety Wins

It's amazing what we were able to accomplish when the shop floor personnel were engaged and involved. Of course, not everyone embraced our new safety culture. It would have been nice to have 100% buy-in and participation, but that is unlikely to happen. Truth be told, we probably had the 20/80 rule at work here. I would guess that about 20% of our hourly workers were driving 80% of our safety efforts. However, over 90% completed kaizen safety projects and got safety T-shirts.

The teams began sharing their efforts. Let's suppose that the average team was made up of twenty people (They varied in size based on department). Maybe only four team members were coming up with most of the team's safety projects, but they were getting buy-in from all team members and sharing the workload in doing the projects.

No team project could be done without their team getting behind it. So even though it was just a few coming up with the projects, most team members participated and would share the credit as the head of the project. The benefits of this sharing were amazing. It created camaraderie, fostered team pride, and brought about stronger work relationships within and between teams. A team would often need the support of a team in a different department, and they would collaborate on projects.

In one department, a team member had the idea of printing a paper sign that said, "STOP - THINK - ACT." Stop was printed red, Think was yellow, and Act was green. With his team's permission, he taped one of these signs wherever an accident in their department occurred. This happened often, as this was one of the high-accident areas in our factory.

Other departments saw this and liked the idea, so from its design, we had small magnetic signs made. We used these throughout our facility, with one magnetic sign placed wherever an accident or near miss occurred. This then spread to other facilities around the world.

Since our factory is part of a global company, we often host visitors from around the world. Our "Stop – Think - Act" signs were noticed, and the idea was borrowed. In 2010, I visited some of our factories in China. As I entered one factory, I saw a large banner that had our familiar red, yellow, and green "STOP-THINK-ACT" written on it in English and Mandarin. It has also been used in one of our factories in Indonesia and many other sites around the world.

This one employee idea spread throughout our factory and around the world! How do you think that person feels about seeing his idea take off like that? If you guessed pretty darn good…you would be correct! I wonder how many people have been kept safe or influenced by his simple idea.

CHAPTER 12

Safe Work Environments

To create and maintain a safe work environment, certain components must be in place. If any of these are missing, frustration quickly sets in. When an employee begins her/his work shift they should have three components in place:

1. A workstation that is well stocked with everything they need to do their job. This includes tools, information, and supplies.

2. A workstation that is clean and safe, with Lean 5-S +1 in place.

3. A process that is under control. They should not begin a shift of firefighting or slaying dragons.

It doesn't matter if the environment is a manufacturing floor, a dairy farm, or a retail outlet. Workers should be able to start their shift with these three components in place. This puts the ball in their court and sets them up for a successful day.

In this type of work environment, workers can make improvements and come up with even better solutions to work-related issues.

Cause and Effect

If the listed three components are not in place, the employee must shift into reaction mode. They are no longer the initiators of action but become the effect! They must regain control and gain the upper hand.

Frustration can quickly zap morale and energy, especially if these conditions are par for the course and describe a typical day. I have observed this scenario, and it is never pretty! The first order of business is to gain control and get these components in place.

Work should not be frustrating on such a basic level. Things will go wrong sometimes in the best work environments, but when you get out of bed in the morning knowing that you are going to have a difficult day at work, it is time to embrace some Lean Manufacturing tools such as standard work and 5S+1.

5S+1 is a continuous improvement tool and an enabler for safety. It will be difficult to have a safe work environment without it.

The 6 S's (5S+1) stand for:

Sort -- Sort out the area and remove items that do not belong. Items you never use should be permanently removed, as in trashed, sold, or given away. No hoarding! Items used rarely should be placed outside the value field (where the main work is done). You want nothing in this area that is not useful and needed for work or safety. This removes clutter. Clutter hides problems.

Shine -- After sorting, clean the area and make it look new. Paint, scrub, and add visuals. Place signs for information, make shadow boards for key items, and make the area as user-friendly as possible. Dirt, oil, dust, etc. also hide problems.

Set -- For the items that are staying, decide on set locations that make sense. You want ease of use and flow. For example, place items near their point of use when possible. Place shadow boards behind tools and other frequently used items as needed. When multiple people work in the same area, stuff seems to get moved out of place and disappear.

Standardize -- Whatever placement or work area configurations you come up with, standardize them in all areas. If employees must learn each area because they are set up differently, there is a problem. A good example of this is our car dashboards. They are all set up in a similar way, so no special training is needed to drive a different vehicle.

Sustain --This may be the most important step, since without a sustainment plan, it will go back to the original condition. This means setting audits and inspections. Each shift should leave their work area the way they find it, which should be clean and set to a standard. BONUS - These inspections can also serve as documented safety inspections if you include the safety items needed on the audit form. These daily inspections are a leading indicator for safety. This is powerful!

Safety -- All through the 5S+1 process, you should be looking for unsafe conditions. I encourage this at the beginning at the Sort phase. Deal with unsafe conditions such as trip hazards, electrical issues, and ergonomics as you uncover them. Use the sustainment audits to make sure conditions stay free of danger.

In addition to providing an attractive, clean, and functional work environment, the real purpose of 6S is to uncover problems. Let's say I visited a friend's house, and she is very neat and organized. If I leave a mark on her carpet, she sees it immediately. If I ignore her coasters and leave a ring on her coffee table, she notices.

Now let's say she comes to my house, and I am a bit of a slob. She can leave marks on the carpet and rings on my tables, and I will never notice because my cleanliness bar is too low.

We need all safety issues to get our attention without having to look for them. That is what 5S+1 can offer. Any work environment or even home can benefit from these practices.

Here is another familiar scenario I have seen in real life. In department "A," there is a workbench used and shared by all shifts. It is covered with gear boxes, tools, rags, and assemblies. A gear box is removed from the equipment and placed on the bench. A new gearbox has been taken out of supply to replace the old one.

The old gear box that sits on the bench needs to be sent off to be rebuilt, but it now blends in with the other stuff and remains unnoticed. Weeks and months have gone by. When will it be noticed? When it is needed...only then will workers find that it was never rebuilt.

In department "B," the same thing happens, but they keep their work bench clean, making sure that the bench is cleared off at the end of each shift. In this department, the gear box is quickly noticed and sent off for a rebuild.

With a good state of 5S+1, problems surface on their own. The environment communicates with you. This makes life much easier. Safety concerns in the workplace will stand out and grab attention. Wish 5S+1, the work environment is now self-monitoring, self-regulating and self-correcting.

Safety Basics

Along with 5S+1 there is the need to make sure other safety basics are in place, such as:

- First aid kits and AEDs

- Water fountains or another drinking water supply

- Fire extinguishers and alarms

- Eye washing stations (as needed)

- Emergency lighting

- Clear exit and shelter signs

- Emergency response plans

- Access to emergency phone numbers

- Emergency exit rout maps

- Signage for shelter rooms. Such as for tornadoes. (Roll call to make sure no one is missing.)

- Safety communication boards

Just as it is up to management to make sure all the necessary safety equipment is provided; workers need to know where these things are. They must be accessible, and workers must know how to use them.

Government safety agencies such as OSHA have guidelines for what safety items are needed for your type of workplace, so refer to them and make sure you are complying. Remember for all identified hazards, the proper control measure must be in place.

For all safety items in your workplace, a system of annual audits will ensure that all safety items are ready for use and in good working condition. Your 5S+1 audits can be used to capture this. All safety items should be listed on the 5S audit form and checked off each day (or each week or whatever interval needed for success). It must follow your health and safety management system and your governing safety enforcement agency.

CHAPTER 13

Emergency Response Plan

An emergency response plan is a list of potential emergencies and the control plans for handling them. The emergency response plan should include all potential emergencies. such as:

- Fire

- Power outage

- Bomb threat

- Severe weather such as tornadoes, earthquakes, hurricanes

- Violence

- Medical emergencies

- Poisoning

- Etc.

Any emergency that could potentially occur should have a plan in place. For high-likelihood scenarios, drills are recommended. For instance, with our factory being in Kansas, we performed tornado drills on all shifts each year. These were important, since each year, without fail, we would have real tornadoes that sent all workers to our basement shelter.

Your emergency response plan should be posted in multiple locations, so it is easily accessible to all. These should be numbered and inspected on a scheduled basis. As plans are improved or changed, the ERPs must be updated.

We made it a point to have an emergency response plan posted next to every phone in our facility. All employees knew this and were trained in their use. This way, an employee could easily also call 911 or use the intercom if required.

We told our employees that when in doubt, they should call 911. We would rather have an emergency vehicle show up and be able to say we had it under control than react too late and put someone at risk.

Your emergency response plan should cover 911 emergencies. We had guidelines in place that required one employee to stay with the injured individual while another alerted a supervisor and yet another went to the parking lot to guide the emergency vehicle to the closest door to respond to the injured person. This worked quite well for us.

Example of Preparedness and Empowerment

One night an employee fell off a piece of equipment and was knocked unconscious. The only supervisor on shift was in another part of the factory. The supervisor was notified via the factory PA system. By the time he walked to the location with the injured employee, emergency medical personnel were also arriving.

One employee who witnessed the accident had alerted others to stay with the injured person while he called 911. He had also sent a person to watch for the ambulance and guide them to the injured employee. The supervisor was called after they had dialed 911 and looked after their fallen coworker. I was proud of how our employees responded. The injured employee had a concussion and received excellent, timely care due to the training of empowered employees. They followed our emergency response plan.

Involve Your Local Fire Department

Work with your local fire department for emergency response. We had our closest fire department visit our facility and tour it once a year. This made them comfortable with our site and built a good relationship between us.

They were able to provide us with tips and guidelines to help them help us. These agencies are usually happy to help in this manner. It will make everyone's experience better should they have to respond to a real emergency.

They become familiar with all our points of entrance and layout of our factory.

We trained all employees to follow safety first in response to emergency situations. We wanted them to error on the side of caution. This meant they were not to risk the safety of themselves or others when facing potential threats.

Fire extinguishers, for example, are meant for very small fires. If the fire is not quite small, call 911.

We told employees we had an agreement with our local fire department; we would not try to put out fires and they would not try to make fluorescent lamps.

Call the professionals. We would rather turn them away after arrival, saying we got it all under control than risk not having them respond in a timely manner.

Head Count

For any evacuation emergency, the most important aspect is head count. We need to make sure all people on the work site are accounted for.

In the event of a fire emergency, the arriving fire fighters will want to know if they are doing a search and rescue versus only putting out the fire. As part of our standard work instructions for these types of emergencies, we had department heads responsible for making sure all their people were accounted for. Lead mechanics on productions lines made sure their people were accounted for. We made sure everyone was part of a group with a leader.

During practice tornado and fire drills we recorded how fast we were able to evacuate and meet in the designated meeting point. We made sure everyone was accounted for.

Make sure your dedicated meeting point is not in the way of emergency vehicles.

All potential emergencies need to have a plan in place. This is a living document and a base line. You should be constantly seeking to improve your emergency preparations.

One potential emergency that you should consider is sudden cardiac arrest. In the next chapter, we will discuss the benefits of an AED program.

CHAPTER 14

AEDs In the Workplace

About 610,000 people die of heart disease in the United States every year. This means 1 in every 4 deaths is from heart disease. Heart disease is the leading cause of death for both men and women.

One item you may want to consider having is an AED - an automated external defibrillator. If you choose to make AEDs available, there are guidelines that must be followed to comply with maintaining a lifesaving device. Since it is a lifesaving device, scheduled inspections must be set and recorded to make sure it is in working order and that the pads and battery are up to date. I once visited a manufacturing site that had only one AED. The battery was dead, and the pads had expired.

I encourage you to consider making this lifesaving equipment available. When we consider workplace emergencies, sudden cardiac arrest is a very real threat.

SCA is one of the leading causes of death and it is a threat we can prepare for.

- EMS treat nearly 300,000 people who suffer cardiac arrest outside the hospital in the U.S. each year according to the American Heart Association. Nearly 325,000 die each year from sudden cardiac arrest

- In cities where defibrillation is provided within 5 to 7 minutes, the survival rate is as high as 30–45 percent

If every community could achieve even a 20 percent survival rate by early bystanders performing CPR and by AED's being more widely available, an estimated 40,000 more lives could be saved each year.

AEDs like Philips Heartstart are designed to be used with zero training. A friend of mine relayed this story to me. He happened to be in an airport and saw a man fall to the ground. The first people gathered could not detect a heartbeat. One of our Philips Heartstart AEDs was mounted on a wall nearby. When they turned it on...it told them step by step what to do. They were able to use it correctly to save the man's life.

Our facility is quite large, and we have five of these staged throughout the factory. All employees were trained in the use of our AEDs. One summer day, we used one of them to save the life of an employee. Not just an employee, a friend.

Sudden Cardiac Arrest and Heart Attack

A heart attack is not the same as SCA. A heart attack is caused by a blockage of one or more of the arteries to the heart. This prevents the heart from receiving enough oxygen-rich blood. Lack of oxygen can cause the heart muscle to become damaged. This can lead to a heart attack.

Sudden cardiac arrest occurs when the electrical system to the heart malfunctions and suddenly becomes very irregular. The irregular heartbeat is unable to deliver blood throughout the body as needed. The victim will soon lose consciousness due to lack of blood in the brain. Death will quickly follow in the absence of emergency treatment.

Ability to Save a Life

Unlike regular defibrillators, an automated external defibrillator (AED) requires little training to use. Many are designed for use with no training at all. These automatically diagnose the heartbeat and will not allow a shock to be given unless needed.

I have performed training sessions with employees where in the beginning of the class I ask how many feel they could use an AED on someone if needed. Typically, few hands go up. After the training session which focusses on AED ease of use, when asked, almost all hands are raised.

Modern AEDs are designed for the untrained individual. They are designed to help the untrained person be able to save a life.

What about Liability?

AEDs are common and easy to use. In most states in the U.S., they are covered under "Good Samaritan" laws. Protection under the Good Samaritan law means the person using the AED was acting in "good faith" as a volunteer responder. They cannot be held civilly liable for harm or death by providing improper or inadequate care.

This law protects individuals from liability for damages that may occur from their use of an AED to save someone's life in an emergency.

AED Program

I highly recommend an AED for your business if you have many employees or customers such as with a restaurant, etc. AEDs can be purchased for around $1000. That's not bad for something that can save your life.

If you decide to make one available, you will need to establish an AED program. Let's face it, if you go to the trouble of having a piece of equipment that can save a life, you should put together a basic program to make sure it is always in order and ready for use.

The AED pads have expiration dates. This is to ensure the adhesive is good and the pads are functional. Make sure you replace the pads as needed. The battery also needs checked and replaced as needed. Some AEDs have a system-check you can cycle through by hitting a button.

The manufacturer's guidelines will tell you how to care for the AED. Because this is a lifesaving device some governing agencies like OSHA may require you maintain records of set inspections. Don't let this detour you from getting one. This is a good thing; we want to make sure our AED is working if we need it. The inspections take only a moment or two.

Monthly checks shall include the following elements:

- Emergency kit supplies

- AED battery life

- AED operation and status

- Pad expiration date

For the emergency kit, I would recommend keeping with the AED:

- Scissors for cutting away clothing

- Paper towels for wiping away sweat quickly

- An extra set of pads

- Aspirin

Place the AED in a location that is marked and accessible, never blocked. Although AEDs are designed so someone with no training, it is a good idea to provide training to workers. They should know how to turn it on and follow the directions. Using an AED will be scary, we are dealing with a life-or-death situation. The more familiar your employees are, the more confident they will feel in an emergency. The more people you have trained, the better. They can work as a team supporting each other.

Consider Making an AED Available

Many people that experience SCA have no known risk factors.

Defibrillation is the only known treatment proven to restore a normal heart rhythm. CPR can buy the victim more time as the AED arrives. CPR will not restore the heart rhythm needed. Defibrillate within three minutes and the chances of survival are 70 percent. After 10 minutes, the chances of survival are negligible.

Purchasing an AED may seem like going overboard for safety, but as the number one killer, shouldn't we be prepared? AEDs save lives and it could be your life it saves.

Overwhelmed

When considering all the aspects involved with keeping workers safe, we can get overwhelmed. It's good to remember you are not alone. Any business with employees deals with these same issues. Network with other safety professionals and support each other. Share best practices and build relationships. This boosts confidence by giving you someone who can help support your safety efforts.

CHAPTER 15

Network

When I became the safety officer for our fluorescent light factory, I began reaching out to other safety professionals immediately. People in the safety field are generally glad to help others achieve safer conditions. I also visited other factories that had good safety programs.

I found that our town has a safety network that meets once a month at a local restaurant for lunch. They had speakers to provide guidance in their fields, including visits from one of our state OSHA representatives.

This local safety network became invaluable to me. It gave me the chance to talk to other safety professionals from local factories and businesses. We shared the same challenges and were glad to share resources and provide support for each other.

Their guidance was extremely helpful. I continued to go to their meetings for all the years I was involved with safety, and I still attend them when I can.

Other businesses are dealing with the same safety issues you are dealing with. People like helping others stay safe. Reach out, and you will most likely be able to help others as you gain insights from their experience.
Reach out to any local businesses that you think can give you some guidance. I have found that almost all companies are willing to share best practices when it comes to safety. Many are proud of their safety programs and want to highlight them to others.

If your town does not have any type of safety network, think about creating one. Why should everyone slay a large dragon in isolation? Working together and sharing experience and safety knowledge can give you tools and insights you may never come across on your own.

Our local safety network filled in the information gap for me on many occasions. It's nice to be able to call up a local safety professional that has dealt with the same issues you're facing. Reach out and network with others for safety.

LinkedIn - LinkedIn has safety groups that provide networking on a massive scale. This is a great resource for gaining information and reaching out to other safety professionals. Forums allow for discussions on safety topics, offering perspective and guidance.

Safeopedia.com is a website which provides up to date information and resources. It also has a strong safety community you can join and access online. I have taken advantage of Safeopedia since 2015 and I belong to its online community. They are a great bunch of people who care about safety and helping others. I have made many new friends via the Safeopedia online community.

CHAPTER 16

Incident Investigations

Despite the best efforts to keep workers safe, what do we do when an accident or near-miss occurs? Investigate, document and create a control measure.

Most safety regulatory agencies and management systems require a thorough investigation to take place following any safety incident. Be sure to check with your regulatory agency to make sure you meet all requirements regarding investigations, reporting and documentation.

The investigation must include these components:
- A complete accident investigation report (listing the details and all contributing factors that lead to the accident. This should include statements from the injured party and any witnesses).

- Evidence validating the statements from those interviewed. This could include photographs of the area or equipment involved. Evidence helps all parties involved understand what caused the accident. Evidence is void of opinion. We want facts.

- A documented Root Cause Analysis. This is a structured approach to finding the true root cause. This verifies that the corrective measures have the best chance at success by focusing on the actual root cause of the accident.

- An identified control measure implemented to avoid a repeat of the accident, you may also need to show that you are monitoring the control measure, and it is working. Validate effectiveness.

I have carried out hundreds of accident investigations. (More than I would have liked) I became very good at capturing the information needed to identify the root cause and implement control measures. I will help you to be able to do the same.

CSI

Time to put on your CSI cap, just like a crime scene investigator; you need to capture all relevant evidence as to the cause of the accident. We need to know what really happened.

Once an accident occurs, it is important to investigate the scene immediately, while the evidence is fresh. Another reason for this is to make sure no one else gets hurt by the same exposed hazard. We want a control measure in place quickly. A short-term fix may be needed, such as a barrier to block off the area until we know it is safe.

Accident Investigation Form

A good accident investigation form can make this process from start to finish much easier. A good accident investigation form will do most of the heavy lifting for you. A good template will list all the information you need. I created a template in MS Word, and we used it for years, making improvements to it over time. If I took pictures as part of the investigation, I inserted these into the word document so they could be referenced as part of a complete report.

The investigation form must capture all needed information including the control measure.

For more information on accident investigations, including a great template, visit Safeopedia and the article: Accident Investigation 101. It will give you much of the information you need to put together a solid accident investigation program.

When possible, I always had the injured party fill out the section explaining what happened. This way, it was in their words. If their writing hand was injured or they could not actually write it themselves, I let them dictate to me and I transcribed it for them. I would treat damage to property and near misses the same. In fact, we used the same form and followed the same process, regardless of injury or no injury.

Not to sound like a broken record about standard work, but standard work should be created covering all aspects of an accident investigation. This would include the items mentioned in the above bullets. When improvements are made to the investigation procedure, revise the standard work instructions.

After a full investigation, perform a root cause analysis. This is very important and why you collected all the accident/incident information. We need to prevent re-occurrence.

Make use of tools like fishbone diagrams and the "five whys" to analyze all the information you collected. Once you have an assigned root cause, you can determine the best control measure to put in place. This should be reviewed with all individuals involved. We also had our safety committee review all the investigations. The safety committee review validated our conclusions as they gave their insight.

Make sure the identified control measure does not interfere with the worker's ability to perform needed tasks. I have always reviewed the suggested corrective actions with those that do the work and department heads before implementation. This goes a long way towards gaining buy-in from those affected by any change.

As part of our standard work, all investigations were reviewed by our safety committee. Safety committee members also were assigned to help with the investigation. This boosted everyone's confidence that we were on the right track.

CHAPTER 17

Results of Our Safety Initiative

In 2009, we cut our OSHA recordable accidents in half! We continued to improve over the next few years. For the first time in our factory's history, our workers were enjoying a safe work environment. No longer was there an expectation of three accidents per week.

The time I had been spending on accident investigations could now be spent driving safety in a more proactive manner. This was much more rewarding for me and everyone else.

Our factory was recognized by Philips with a global safety award after our transformation. We became known as leaders for safety within Philips. This gave me the opportunity to travel to some nice locations to talk about our transformation and what we learned.

What I have outlined in this book is what I have told those I have visited.

Safety First Culture

Why does this safety program work and why will it work for you? I have given this a lot of thought. Our safety program does not rely on rules. It relies on human nature. We took a simple approach that placed people first. Here are the activities we did that created a successful safety-first culture.

People first + structured processes = safety

We put our people first and gave them processes to keep them safe. We acted like a good football coach: Equip, support and celebrate! We equipped our employees with training and resources. We celebrated safety successes often.

We stated safety was our most important measurement and we reinforced it every chance we could. Management took one voice and that was Safety first.

We trained our people in safety basics:

- We taught the difference between hazard and danger. (Danger means you can get hurt, hazard means the danger has been recognized and a control measure is in place for your safety. We can work around hazards all day and never be in danger.)

- How to identify hazards and the associated risks.

- We gave them an understanding about safety control measures to protect them from danger. They needed to see how the control measure protected them and why it needed to stay in place.

We fostered community at work. All employees belonged to a team, and we encouraged them to protect each other. Watch each other's backs and follow the moral safety compass: Would you let one of your adult sons or daughters perform an unsafe act if they were working here? There is no substitute for caring for each other. If employees believe you do not care about them, your safety program will be difficult to promote.

We used kaizen to enable employees to come up with safety projects. We encouraged them to become "Dragon slayers." Once they identified a problem, they could come up with a solution.

We used safety meetings and boards to keep safety momentum going. We constantly gave updates on safety status. We quickly alerted everyone when an accident or near miss occurred. Our safety boards and meetings highlighted safety and health topics.

We tried to keep safety in the forefront in people's minds as we stayed proactive.

We taught about the three motivators regarding our actions and safety:

1. The desire for reward

2. The avoidance of pain

3. The conservation of energy

We had our leaders focus on using the right behavior to encourage and lead. We did not want them to overemphasize production goals at the expense of safety. They had to keep our business on track and move forward without jeopardizing safety.

We learned that engaged workers can come up with amazing solutions to issues.

We created our five-step safety formula and promoted it constantly. (On safety boards, in meetings, and on wallet cards we gave everyone)

Fivefold safety formula:

1. Watch for and avoid Shortcuts

2. Watch for and avoid Snap decisions

3. Watch for and avoid Complacency

4. Actively look for unsafe conditions

5. Actively look for unsafe behaviors

Core components for driving safety are:

- Understand human nature regarding taking risks physically to protect ourselves emotionally.

- Recognize people as our greatest asset and build a sense of community.

- Invest time and money in promoting safety (This should never stop; we invest in what we care about).

- Implement Lean Manufacturing tools like Kaizen, Standard Work Instructions and 5S+1 (I do not believe we would have been successful in our safety program without these lean tools).

- Train and empower your employees, make them dragon slayers and safety professionals about their work.

- Encourage employees to help drive safety efforts. Ask for their help often and recognize their value and contribution.

- Network, ask for help from other safety professionals.

- Make sure management has one message and one voice about safety which is safety comes first

- Make the most of accident investigations – collect data, find the root cause of each incident. Keep good records and use this information to implement improvements.

- Pro-actively seek compliance with governing safety agencies.

- Use your "Moral Safety Compass," If you would not allow a grown daughter or son perform a dangerous work activity, don't let anyone else perform it.

- Follow the safety pattern: Emotional safety, professional safety, physical safety. Protect employees on all three levels.

- Embrace the safety performance cycle: Hazard analysis and risk assessments, safety training, provide time for safety inspections.

- Celebrate success! Look for reasons to celebrate safety success and celebrate   often.

Safety will always require effort and provide a challenge. Complacency is so easy! If management shifts emphasis away from safety and makes employees feel that the business performance targets are once again the all-important driver, the safety culture will suffer.

Your employees want to help hit company goals and targets. It is in their best interest for the company to prosper and succeed. They must be able to stay safe while achieving needed company goals. No one wants to get hurt at work. Our job is to support them by providing safety training, safety management systems and celebrating their safety successes often.

In the months when we had special projects on the shop floor that overshadowed safety, our accident rates started to climb back up. We are naturally competitive and people working on a project want to succeed. This is why safety must be highlighted during these events.

One of our project managers started holding safety meetings every day with his team. Before they were allowed to start work on the new project, they were reminded about safety. It sets the tone for the day's work. They started a large project with lots of potential risks. As a result of his focus on safety, there were no injuries to his team during its successful completion.

Are Zero Accidents Possible?

This is a popular topic I see on LinkedIn and with safety groups. It is normally phrased as a question such as "Are zero accidents possible?" or should the goal for workplace safety be "Zero accidents?"

When someone would ask me if I thought zero accidents were possible in our factory, I would say possible yes…probable no. I may have been wrong. Although we have never gone for a year with zero accidents, we had departments, shifts and workers that did go accident-free. We also had other factories within Philips experiencing long stretches with no accidents. These factories were also implementing a safety-first culture.

At the start of 2009, we decided we would set our safety goal at achieving a 50% reduction in OSHA recordable accidents. Since we were experiencing one per week, we thought that was a pretty good goal. We were extremely happy to hit that goal by the end of 2009.

Our injury rate continued to drop in 2010 and 2011. In 2012 we shifted attention from safety. We had some major projects going on and safety slid backwards, and accidents rose. When management noticed this trend, they reminded all workers that safety still must be first. We followed our safety basics we established in 2009. 2013 had the lowest accident rate in our factories' history.

Looking closer at safety in our factory, we came across some noteworthy observations. We had one shift go for an entire year without any OSHA recordable injuries. This was amazing. Our factory production was divided into four crews working on twelve-hour shifts.

Our Four Production Shifts:

A1 Shift – Monday through Wednesday and every other Sunday, working from 6 am to 6 pm
B1 Shift – Monday through Wednesday and every other Sunday, working from 6 pm to 6 am

A2 Shift – Thursday through Saturday and every other Sunday, working from 6 am to 6 pm

B2 Shift - Thursday through Saturday and every other Sunday, working from 6 pm to 6 am

This meant a fourth of our lamp production workforce had no OSHA recordable accidents for a year! We did not think that was possible.

The shift that accomplished this was our least preferred shit with our least senior employees. This was our B2 shift. Since it was nights and weekends, it had the highest turnover as employees could not wait to get on a shift with better hours.

When I looked deeper into this shift and why it was so successful with safety, I made some interesting discoveries. The night shift supervisor promoted safety heavily. He did not just "talk the talk."

Employees on the night shift knew he valued their safety. He actively watched for unsafe acts and conditions. He was seen as someone that was proactive about safety and the wellbeing of his employees. He had strong loyalty from his employees.

Since the night shift production supervisor had been a lead production mechanic himself, he knew the dangers employees faced. He was able to discourage activities such as working on running equipment or disregarding personal protective equipment.

This night shift was not the only safety champions we noticed experiencing zero accidents. We also had our glass department go for over a year with no OSHA recordable injuries. This was our highest injury department.

This department was where the glass was made from sand and other materials. This department had over 50 individuals working there. It also used high-speed equipment.

When I conducted a study on their success, I found many of the same factors that were present on the night shift; the glass department management team proactively promoted safety. They celebrated safety wins more than any other department. They held more team meetings which promoted safety. They had the highest level of leading indicators regarding safety.

When they achieved a set amount of time during the year with no OSHA recordable injuries, they would celebrate. They encouraged safety projects from all glass team members. They often had more safety kaizen projects than any other department.

One of these safety projects was the development of the STOP-THINK-ACT signs that had spread through the factory and to China, Mexico, and Indonesia.

The proactive approach taken on the B2 shift and in the Glass Department lowered their accident rates. They were proving that zero accidents were possible. We had one more example of zero accidents to study.

Our factory had over 400 hourly employees and many had been working in our factory for over 20 years, some over 40. We had employees that had never experienced an accident that required outside medical attention. (An OSHA Recordable injury) We had employees that worked accident-free. When I interviewed these employees and observed their work habits, I noticed once again they valued safety and tended to be more proactive than many of their co-workers.

I am betting you have met these types of people; they always wear seatbelts, actively look out for the safety of others, always use the right tools and keep an organized, clean work area. They wear PPE as required. They follow our five-fold approach to safety. The value safety as part of their professionalism.

The realist in me wants to say that zero accidents is not possible but, in our factory, the B2 shift, our glass department and many senior employees would prove me wrong. Zero accidents may not be possible, but it should always be the goal. We must realize that safety and the journey to zero accidents is a guiding star and not a distant shore. We will never arrive. There is always more we can do and farther we can go. Seek improvement over perfection.

CHAPTER 18

Safety Management System

"We do not rise to the level of our goals. We fall to the effectiveness of our systems."
Scott Adams

Systems give us a structure to make sure what needs to happen does happen. You need a safety management system in place that you can rely on to keep employees safe and keep your organization compliant with all governing regulatory requirements such as OSHA.

Your safety management system is made up of six categories:

1. **People focus:** Make a commitment to put people first. People must be as important as profit and performance. They are the means to the end of making a lasting profit. All workers want to be successful at their work and know businesses need profit. Problems and dilemmas arise when profit and performance are desired at the expense of worker safety. (Remember the moral safety compass) Loyalty and caring will drive engagement, performance and profits.

2. **Hazard Identification and control:** We need activities in place to constantly flush out hazards and create controls for them. This is the foundation of worker safety. Use hazard identification risk assessment forms and keep them up to date. Do risk analysis of all work tasks, equipment

and work environments. Use a "Last Minute Risk Assessment" form for new projects, and non-routine work.

3. **Safety Training:** New Hire safety training and annual safety training are required to keep employees safe. Hazard identification and control does no good unless people are trained to understand them. We must develop a safety program that equips, supports and celebrates employee safety. Your safety program is only as affective as your safety training is.

4. **Safety Inspections:** Situations change constantly; therefore, safety inspections are needed to flush out danger. This includes safety inspections for forklifts, hand tools, 6S audits, etc. (These must be documented and saved) Set different levels of safety inspections to take place each shift, daily, weekly, monthly and annually.

5. **Incident Investigations:** Injuries, property damage, and near misses need to be investigated in a timely manner. The goal is to prevent a recurrence. When an accident occurs, we must learn all we can from it. This is the silver lining. Danger has been uncovered and can be addressed.

6. **Documentation and Reporting:** Documentation and reporting is how you prove your safety system is in place and effective. Records must be saved as evidence of compliance with safety laws. This is one reason why Sign-in sheets for safety training are important. Severe accidents such as amputations, in-patient hospitalization or fatality must be reported to OSHA within 24 hours. Make sure

you are aware of all governing agency reporting requirements such as the OSHA 300 LOG.

Safety is either proactive or it is inactive. If your safety management system is in place and active, you can be confident you are doing your best to keep everyone safe. When you see any of these areas slipping, it means your commitment to safety is slipping and accidents are more likely to occur. Audit your safety management system annually.

Here is an example of a safety management system outline. It captures all six categories listed above. Your SMS should be reviewed and updated at least annually. Your SMS is a leading indicator for safety.

Safety Management System Outline Example

1. **People Focus**
   a. Safety Policy in place and posted stating your commitment to safety.
   b. Safety committee in place and making a difference by ensuring safety stays proactive. The safety committee:
      i. Reviews all incidents.
      ii. Reviews all SMS activities.
      iii. Use data to focus on safety efforts.
      iv. Ensures recognition and celebration for safety achievements.
   c. Strong safety leadership throughout organization.
      i. Managers and leaders are viewed as safety champions.
      ii. "Safety-First," is not just a slogan. WALK THE TALK.
   d. High engagement in the work environment.

       i.   Each department performs its own safety inspections. These are documented and saved.

      ii.   Safety ownership belongs to the employees. Management is accountable for safety, and the employees are responsible for safety.

  e. Leading indicators focus on all safety key performance indicators.

       i.   Safety behavior observations.

      ii.   Safety Kaizens. (Safety projects and improvements.)

     iii.   5S+1 inspections.

     iv.   Safety inspections as required including facility, tools, and equipment.

      v.   Safety training (Invest time in equipping people to stay safe).

     vi.   Safety committee meetings.

    vii.   Safety celebrations.

   viii.   Safety communication and employee involvement. (Employee engagement.)

  f. Safety is accepted as the number one priority. Safe employees that are cared for engage more. There is less turnover, and higher profitability, which is sustainable.

2. Hazard Identification and control

  a. Hazard identification process is in place with up-to-date HIRAs. (Hazard Identification Risk Assessment) Updated often based on information from incidents and inspections. This is the first step of the safety continuous performance cycle.

  b. SAO and JSA updated for all tasks, work areas and in use. Update along with HIRAs.

       i.   SAO: Safety Awareness Orientation. This is a list of hazards and control measures in place to protect workers. It is based on the work they will be doing and the work environment. This can be reviewed with each employee after hiring or transferring to a new workplace.

    ii. JSA: Job Safety Analysis. All work tasks are analyzed for potential danger. The hazards are listed along with the control measures for safety. SAOs are created from the information uncovered by the Job Safety Analysis.

c. Strong safety training program in place.

d. Evidence of affective safety performance cycle in place.

    i. Hazard identification and controls

    ii. Safety Training

    iii. Safety Inspections

    iv. Start over. Use all safety information learned to update hazard identification, training and inspections... (Plan, Do, Check, Act)

3. **Safety Inspections (list all inspections)**

    a. Shift & daily (forklift, 6S, Hoists, slings, harnesses, ladders, etc.)

    b. Weekly inspections, if needed. (Check with your industry's best practices.)

    c. Monthly, if needed. (facility inspections, storm water, accumulation area, etc.)

    d. Quarterly Inspections: These can include a variety of checks. Review the safety management system overall. Are you slipping anywhere?

    e. Annual (yearly) Hoist, slings, noise and air quality, ergonomics, safety training, storm pond, OSHA 300 log report, etc. Equipment such as slings and cranes need a third party inspection annually.

4. **Safety Training (identify all required safety training) This is based on your HIRA.** OSHA can also provide you with information regarding safety training topics and requirements. You have two categories regarding safety training topics. Awareness and performance based. People that work around forklifts need to be trained in all aspects

of working around forklifts such as keeping a safe distance from them. Using walking pathways and stopping at forklift intersections. This is awareness training. However, this training does not enable them to drive a forklift. To drive a forklift, they need deeper training on how to operate a forklift. They need a level of training that certifies them as competent to drive a forklift safely. They receive a forklift license. This is performance training.

a. **Awareness training examples**
    i. Bloodborne Pathogen
    ii. HIRA, JSA & SAO use and understanding
    iii. Safety culture & behavior-based safety
    iv. Active shooter and workplace violence
    v. PPE, ergonomics, lifting, slips-trips-falls.
    vi. Heat-related illness
    vii. Emergency responses include extreme weather, workplace violence, sudden cardiac arrest, etc.
    viii. SDS and chemicals handling. (include any hazardous waste)
    ix. Fire emergencies and Fire extinguishers
    x. Lock Out Tag Out (LOTO)

b. **Performance training examples**
    i. LOTO – to perform LOTO
    ii. Hot work – Anyone doing hot work such as welding
    iii. Respirator – Anyone that must wear a respirator
    iv. Confined space – for working in confined spaces
    v. Forklift – License program
    vi. Hoist – Crane operation license
    vii. Personal fall arrest systems – for working at elevated height
    viii. Bloodborne Pathogen – Part of first responder
    ix. First aid and CPR training for first response providers

c. **Drills**
    i. Emergency response drills

1. Tornado, AED, chemical spill, Etc.
ii. Fire Drill – must show the names of all employees that participated. Must have 100 % participation.

5. **Incident Investigations (Structure investigations and capture root cause. Use your safety committee and others for accountability and accuracy.)**
    a. Injuries
    b. Near miss
    c. Property damage
    d. Work related illnesses
    e. Environmental issues

6. **Documents and reporting**
    a. HIRAS, SAO, JSA. These should be viewed as living documents and updated as needed.
    b. Standard work instructions (Quality system document control in place.)
    c. Training documentation included:
        i. Topic of training
        ii. Trainer
        iii. Training materials
        iv. Sign-in sheet
        v. Proof of training effectiveness if necessary such as a test and hands on training for competency review.
    d. Investigations: Keep all investigation review forms.
    e. OSHA 300 Log (Immediately record incidents in OSHA log after they happen)

My Goal with this Book

The ball is now on your court. My goal with this book is to provide readers with a short, direct, and to-the-point guide for improving worker safety. This means the next step is yours. This book has the information I wish had available to me when I began my journey in workplace safety in 2008.

I did my best to include information I would provide you if I were working alongside you to build a safety program. I encourage you to network with other safety professionals, become familiar with your government's safety regulations (OSHA website) and use safety websites such as Safeopida.com.

Much of this book is based on a case study. It is from our successful implementation of a safety-first culture in our Philips Lighting factory. I also had the pleasure of sharing our accomplishments with other Philips factories and seeing them implement many of our ideas. I am proud of what we accomplished regarding worker safety. I honestly can't think of any part of my work life that has been more challenging or rewarding than being part of this transformation.

In 2013, I turned over our safety program to a new safety manager. My time was still divided between safety and my other duties as the senior trainer and being a project leader. Management wanted a safety manager fully dedicated to worker health and safety. We had a good management team that wanted to continue to improve our safety culture.

I was proud of the safety program our new manager took over. It was a fully developed health and safety management system which had a good track record for sustainable safety. We were OSAS 18001 certified (a health and safety management certification developed in Europe). This was a long way from what I inherited in 2008.

I met many safety heroes while working for Philips/Signify. Philips promotes itself as a "Health and Well-being" company, and that is what they truly are. On May 16th, 2018, Philips Lighting changed its name to Signify. The name change was part of the company's repositioning in the lighting market. The name Signify was chosen because the company believes light can be an intelligent language that conveys meaning and connects people. Signify is a leader in the development of LED lighting systems and using LED lighting to improve the quality of life.

Safety begins with commitment to people. Safety first means putting people first. This is a community. Do your employees come first? If asked, would they say management values them and cares about their safety? This is where you begin.

Information in this book has been shared with many other safety professionals and much of it has been successfully used to improve safety in different locations and businesses. My sincere hope is that you found some gold safety nuggets you can implement to improve safety or at least gain some food for thought.

Train your dragon slayers and I wish you happy slaying.

I WANT TO HEAR FROM YOU

If this book was helpful, please take a moment and write a quick review on Amazon. Just one or two sentences are fine, and I will be always in your debt. You are helping promote worker safety.

Thank you for purchasing this book. I want to know what you think. Let me know about your experience regarding worker health and safety initiatives. If you implement an idea that is successful in improving safety for your work environment, please share it with me. I am also happy to answer workplace safety questions.

You can contact me via LinkedIn or reach out to me via email at bryan@safeopedia.com

ABOUT THE AUTHOR

Bryan McWhorter is a safety professional with sixteen years of experience in driving and teaching safety. Bryan gained his knowledge and experience as the safety officer and Senior Trainer for Philips Lighting. Now it's called Signify. Philips/Signify is a strong health and well-being company that promotes a safety-first culture.

Bryan was involved in creating a successful safety culture resulting in a 50% reduction in OSHA recordable accidents in the first year. The program continued to have a strong impact in the following years. Bryan's responsibilities included providing and tracking needed safety training, performing hazard assessments, and performing all accident investigations.

Bryan's books on Amazon:

- The Lean Business Model: Our lean journey continues.

- Dragon Slayer Manual: How to deal with problems from the perspective of a dragon slayer.

- The Ultimate Guide to 5S+1: Create a visual workplace and surface problems

- Ultimate Tae Kwon Do: A training guide for martial arts.

- How to Improve Workplace Safety

- Public Speaking with No Fear: 3 Steps to remove anxiety and control fear.

- Where Are All the Gentlemen? Where Are All the Heroes?

- Introduction to Lean Manufacturing: The road to continuous improvement.

- Do You Work for a 10-Year-Old? A Survival guide for dealing with an immature boss.

Schedule Bryan to speak at your next conference

Bryan has spoken on safety throughout the U.S. and in China, Canada, Mexico, Ireland, and Aruba. His practical experience gives him a unique perspective for improving safety. For more information, please refer to Bryan's LinkedIn profile, YouTube or through Safeopedia.

APPENDIX

I purposely kept this book short and to the point, trying to lay out the gold nuggets I uncovered while improving safety at Philips/signify. I did not want to get bogged down with definitions for safety terms such as LOTO or what is a hearing conservation program?

There are many great websites filled with awesome safety goodness including definitions of safety terms. Here are a few, I would recommend:

https://www.safeopedia.com/
https://www.osha.gov/
https://www.osha.gov/international/

When I became the safety officer at Philips, I spent a great deal of time reaching out to safety professionals locally and on the web. I found most to be very gracious and helpful, as we all share a common goal...keep people safe at work.

Reach out to safety professionals near you and you will be amazed at the help and resources they provide. I am always glad to help keep others safe.

Acknowledgements

Special thanks go to:

Thanks, Michelle, for putting up with me disappearing behind a computer for long hours.

Andre Pilon, Nahrin Dowds, Nicole Bergstrom and Linda Schlafer. Thanks for your suggestions, guidance, friendship and encouragement. Special thanks to Jamie Young and Scott Cuthbert of Safeopedia for allowing me the opportunity to be part of the Safeopedia family.

I also want to thank these safety professionals for sharing your knowledge and friendship with me - Luis Alvarado, Richard Mikkers, Marc Van Deursen, Piet van Eekelen, Andrew McKenzie and Hennie Pouwels.